William H. Fremantle

The Gospel of the Secular Life

Sermons Preached at Oxford - With a Prefatory Essay

William H. Fremantle

The Gospel of the Secular Life
Sermons Preached at Oxford - With a Prefatory Essay

ISBN/EAN: 9783337160203

Printed in Europe, USA, Canada, Australia, Japan

Cover: Foto ©Lupo / pixelio.de

More available books at **www.hansebooks.com**

THE

GOSPEL OF THE SECULAR LIFE.

Sermons Preached at Oxford.

WITH A

PREFATORY ESSAY.

BY

THE HON. W. H. FREMANTLE,

LATE FELLOW OF ALL SOULS;
RECTOR OF ST. MARY'S, BRYANSTON SQUARE, AND CANON OF CANTERBURY.

NEW YORK

CHARLES SCRIBNER'S SONS

1883

To

THE UNIVERSITY OF OXFORD,

AND ESPECIALLY TO ITS YOUNGER MEMBERS

IN WHOM LIES SO MUCH OF HOPE FOR

THE FUTURE OF THE CHURCH OF ENGLAND,

THIS WORK IS DEDICATED.

CONTENTS.

———◆———

Prefatory Essay.

THESE sermons are published as an attempt to direct Christian thought into a new channel, its great, not to say paramount, concern with the general, common, or secular life of mankind. The Christian Church is a great power, and nowhere more so than in this country. But it appears hardly conscious of its true strength. It concerns itself with public worship, with pulpit instruction, and with works of beneficence of various kinds, and with the extension of the range of these forms of activity. But the general, common, and secular life lies almost outside its purview. Church work and Church influence are commonly spoken of as if they were something lying apart from the life of science, or art, or politics. And the convictions of men on these subjects are apt to be formed almost without reference to Christianity. Those who lead in these departments are consequently apt, whether they are or are not professedly religious men, to hold an ambiguous position towards the Church. There is in the present day, among men of culture in England, little that can be called scoffing at Christian doctrine; and the attitude of the best minds towards the Christian system generally, if it is often that of hesitancy, is rarely that of denial. But

meanwhile the real interests of men are apt to lie in a
region which Christian teaching hardly touches. Nor
is the phenomenon which we are observing to be
explained by the contrast between worldliness and
godliness. It is rather this—that the decisive and
directing power over men's consciences is not felt to
lie within the Church's sphere, so that, as has been
recently said, the great secular influences form new
religions. Christianity becomes a specialism and a
small affair in the presence of other absorbing objects
of interest, instead of being the supreme spiritual
influence which elevates and harmonises all the
spheres of human life.

It is not necessary to disparage the ordinary work
of the Church. We may rather believe that that work
would gain in width and in vigour from the direction of thought which is here proposed. If Christianity were felt to be intimately concerned with the
general, common, and secular life, its worship would
be much more real, as responding to the wants of all.
Its schemes of beneficence would gain in vigour and
in manliness, because they would be part of the
general direction of human life, and they would not
shrink from contact with the State. And the
Church's teaching especially would take a wider
range. Even the teaching which bears upon ritual
would be coloured by the conviction that the Christ
with whom the prayers and sacraments unite men is
the spiritual centre of the life of mankind and of the
universe. The dogmas would pass into principles;

they would be found to be expressions for the deepest feelings and convictions of the actual life of men, and their significance would gain a new force and colour from each fresh discovery of truth in whatever department. The teaching as to the world to come also would be more closely connected with the moral life here ; it would be the constant background of the picture, a sustaining hope developing itself in a happy present energy.

Those who look thoughtfully into the future may safely leave public worship, instruction, and beneficence to the action of existing forces. The need for them is felt very generally. They are, for the most part, under the charge of competent men, and the mind of Christians is set upon them ; so that the further extension and the gradual changes which they require, the pruning away of excesses, the introduction of lay control, may be regarded as ensured. There is hardly an object of this kind for which some special society does not exist. But that which is needed, and for lack of which Christianity languishes, is a wider outlook, a determination to look the world in the face without misgiving or mistrust, to spiritualise and to harmonise, to foster and to inspire, the various spheres and interests which the Providence of God opens to the men of our day.

It has already been pointed out that, for lack of intercourse with these spheres and interests of secular life, Christianity is in danger of neglect if not of hostility from without, and of shrivelling up into littleness within.   There is another phenomenon which must not be neglected—the divisions among Christians.   It is felt, on the one hand, that the divisions have no sufficient ground of conviction, that they are in fact to a great extent an anachronism, and that there is a real unity independent of them, which is struggling to gain expression.   Men are a little ashamed of these divisions, and of the fact that Christianity is a cause of disagreement rather than of unity in the world, especially in the political life.   But on the other hand there is a kind of impotence which makes them fall back helplessly into sectarianism, at least into that modified sectarianism which is content with outward courtesy without healing the division, and which is thus liable to the reproach of want of principle.   Men cannot frankly discuss their differences without sliding again into the grooves of the old and effete controversies. The surest way to get rid of this sectarianism is to find new ground which is unaffected by it.   So long as modes of worship, and the government of the clergy, and the little interests of congregations, or the reduction of religious ideas to abstract and disputable propositions, are looked upon as the main business of Christianity, there is no way out of sectarianism.   But when Christians find out that their main business is to promote truth in all departments of human knowledge, and love in all the relations of human life, and that they have a concern also in

all that beautifies and refines human existence, and
that all the energy of their faith in God and in
Christ is needed to sustain the progress of mankind,
they will find out also that the ground of their discord recedes into its natural littleness, and that the
faith by which they all are actuated is a great
moral power, as to the possession and use of which
there is no controversy.

The secular life of modern Europe in its higher
aspects may be divided into three great departments:
that of Science—chiefly though not exclusively re-
presented in men's present thoughts by physical
science—that of Art, and that of Politics. It exhibits
also certain ruling ideas or tendencies, of which the
most prominent are Free Criticism, Democratic
Equality, and Progress. Each of these is apt to
claim entire independence, and at times to rise in
opposition to the received Christianity and the
claims of the Church; and a conflict is thus set up,
which on both sides would be described somewhat as
follows. Natural science, it may be said, especially as
inspired by the doctrine of evolution, seems to leave
no room for miracle, no room even for a creator, in
the sense usually given to the word—that is, one who
has made the world out of nothing, and sustains it
ab extra; and, what is more, the pursuit of natural
science seems so absorbing as to fill up the whole
soul, and to leave no room for the common moral
wants, for the sense of sin, and the need of redemption. The votary of art, again, it may be said, claims

to be free and separate. He resents the idea that he is
bound by moral restrictions, such as the early painters
and musicians acknowledged. This is specially seen
in the revived love of the Greek form of culture, and
admiration of the Renaissance. The life of art stands
in contrast with the moral and religious life. So
also the political development, which demands
equality, and frets against authority, has its own
principles of action. Religion is from above, it is said,
dogmatic, authoritative, unchanging; but modern
political life goes its own way, each man and each
section claiming room for their own full development, and the whole passing unfettered "down the
ringing grooves of change." Criticism, again, is
erected into a system which demands recognition
everywhere. No institution, no received custom or
opinion, can be withdrawn from its unabashed gaze.
"I know nothing as holy," said Strauss; "I know
only the true." In any case, the demand is that our
statements should be undogmatic; but is not theology made up of dogmas? If, again, the assertion of
equality is to have its full issue, does not this directly
contravene the privilege allotted hitherto to superiority or goodness in its various forms? And
yet has not the government of God, as set forth in
the Bible, been conducted on the principle of election
and of graded subjection? Lastly, if progress is to
go on incessantly, what goal can be fixed for it?
and is it not, as far as religion is concerned, a progress of negation?

This short statement, which the reader will expand from his own experience, may suffice to set before us the main tendencies of the secular life, and the special difficulties connected with it in our day. The remarks now to be made upon them will be entirely from the standpoint of a Christian teacher.

There are four different ways of dealing with the subject.

First, it may be said by some men that the Church and its ministers, and earnest Christians generally, have nothing to do with these things. "Let us perform our duties," it may be said, "and let the world go its own way. If we are to exert any influence on it, it must be by the spectacle which we present of earnest devotion to our own proper work of prayer, teaching, and beneficence. These will in due time have their effect." This view finds some countenance from the fact that many of those who adopt this course do often, by their simple piety, win a large and beneficial influence. It is far better to have no view at all about science or art or politics than to take a wrong view. And those who are absorbed in secular interests will often feel more sympathy, because they are more left in peace, in the presence of men of simple unquestioning piety than in the presence of those who are earnestly working out the problem of Christian influence in the world. But there are great dangers in such a course. First, it tends to make religion a mere department of life, instead of being the supreme moral power. Next, when men are ignorant of each other they usually suspect and misunderstand each other; and so it is apt to happen with systems of life which thus ignore each other. Thirdly, those who try to ignore the secular life, however simple they may be, are apt to become a prey to those who do not ignore it, but take a wrong view of it; and thus it comes to pass that the Church system of our day, though full of earnestness and doing much good work, is drifting more and more into clericalism. Lastly, the fatal contrast is thus reproduced, which, except where it is taken as a convenient distinction and as expressing a division of labour, is wholly unchristian, between things sacred and things secular. The only contrast known to Christianity is between good and evil. Christ came not to condemn the world, but to save it; and "the world" which is condemned by Him is not the world as secular, but the world as wicked and selfish. The effort of Christians must be not to condemn nor to ignore, but to save.

Secondly, there are those who admit that the secular life has its place and its rights, but who yet dread it as a disturbing and usurping influence. They would, if it were possible, wish back the time when science hardly existed and art was the servant of devotion. They accept the Reformation, and even perhaps the English Revolution; but the reforming and liberal movements of the present day, in which the spirit of the Reformation and the Revolution lives before us again, they fly from with terror. Criticism is to be accepted as dealing with ecclesiastical, but not with Biblical questions. Or, again, the democratic spirit is admitted in politics, but must on no account be allowed to touch the organisation of the Church. Newton's discoveries, though resisted as contrary to Scripture in the beginning of the eighteenth century, are almost held as divine; but Darwin's theories in the middle of the nineteenth are dangerous. This is the attitude of compromise. It has no principle on which it is based. It asserts again and again what it has afterwards to give up. It yields step by step what it had professed to hold as the most important principles or institutions, and, like a bribe paid to an invader, it invites a renewal of the attack. The fault of this mode of raising the question is fundamentally the same as that of the first, namely, that it presumes an antagonism which is fictitious between the Church and the world, the secular and the religious life, and confounds the world as secular and natural with the world as wicked and selfish. But it has a special danger of its own, in that it constantly raises needless controversy and ill-humour, and that it presents the Church and Christianity as a feeble and feminine being dragged hither and thither against its will, rather than as one possessed with the dignity of truth and the assurance of universal empire.

Thirdly, we have the reconciliationists, those who look upon the various secular systems and tendencies

as independent powers, possibly as new forms of·
religion,* which they hope may one day be shown
not to be antagonistic to Christianity. There is on
the one hand the expression of a certain alarm, and on
the other the hope, more or less confident and reasoned,
that the alarm may prove to be needless. The
danger of such an attitude is that it hardly presents a
sufficient basis for action. It hopes for such a basis
rather than gives it us. There is also the danger that
it is apt to take the two supposed antagonists as they
are at a given time, and to form between them a kind
of armistice rather than a durable peace, an armistice
which may fail to meet the next demand of the secular
life. Such an attitude can hardly be avoided in a
period of transition. But it does not present the resting-
place which we need in the presence of the changes of
opinion, the "shaking of the things which are made,"
and their possible removal. Christian teachers cannot help requiring a more confident position from
which to preach to mankind.

That more confident position, we may venture to
believe, is accessible to us. There is a way of dealing
with the problem different from the three which have
been described. This fourth and better way takes

* The work of the author of "Ecce Homo" on Natural Religion has
done a good service in exhibiting the many points of contact between
Christianity as commonly held (or as slightly modified) and the secular
systems which he so vividly describes. But the conclusion which
seems to be the proper result of his work, is rather aimed at and
hoped for than expressed, and the work has therefore appeared to
many as hesitating and disappointing.

as its starting-point not the appearance of disunion,
but the conviction of an original and a final unity.
The supposed antagonism between religion and the
secular life is not one which those who believe in
God ought to recognise. It is a form of dualism,
with this difference—that the old dualism was of
good and evil, this of two forms of good. But goodness is all one, and it is all divine and Christian.
Why should we separate from each other the various
manifestations of the same spirit? No believer in
God can really doubt that every pure and unselfish
development of human energy is consonant with the
will and purpose of God ; nor that humanity and the
world are component parts of one great Unity ; nor
that the elevation of humanity to its noblest and best
estate must be the aim of every man who lives in
earnest. And if there are those who think that religion is the enemy of science or art or the political
life, or of the free exercise of criticism, or of political
equality, or of progress, we must endeavour to undeceive them, just as we must undeceive religious
men who imagine that any of these tendencies are
in themselves anti-religious. Whether we say that
God made the world as a watchmaker makes a watch,
or, with more humility, confine ourselves to observing
the unity of the world and of humanity, and the development of this unity, we cannot doubt that the
supreme power which we call God is Himself at
work in every sphere of existence. When the Posi-
tivist says that his Trinity is Humanity, the World,

B

and Space, he announces the same conviction which is expressed in the words, "God who made the world and all that is therein," so far, at least, as this unity is concerned. No doubt the metaphysical question may be raised whether this implies a making or ordering of the world *ab extra* or *ab intra*. But such a question does not necessarily affect Christian Theism. What, then, does this unity imply? Certainly the unity of the development of mankind in all its relations to the universe, of which it forms the crown; the unity, therefore, of the spheres of science, art, political life, under the one divine principle or power, the acknowledgment of which constitutes theology and religion. Using, therefore, without any needless assumption, the ordinary Christian language, we may say that no such antagonism as that between the religious and secular life ought to be possible, since God made the world, and combined its component parts in one.

Has, then, the appearance of Christ created this antagonism? The Christian belief, on the contrary, is expressed in the words, "All things were made by Him (the Word who was made flesh in Christ)," and "In Him was life, and the life was the light of men, . . . the true light that lighteth every man." How can any one who believes this consider that any human excellence is strange to Christ, or that there is anything exclusive in Him who is One with God? We must go further, and assert that wherever any human excellence is to be found, there He is present as the

inspirer of it. Wherever such excellence is pursued
without the recognition of Him, there is an unconscious Christianity; wherever there is such excellence
together with this recognition, there is a conscious
Christianity. But even where the spring of the excellence is unrecognised, or through ignorance denied,
there should be on the part of Christians a hearty
appreciation of the excellence itself. This should
be an elementary article of belief, that all human excellence is essentially divine, and essentially Christian.

It follows from this that Christians should be
interested in and should foster all that is excellent
in science or art or political life as that which is
their proper business. They should seek first to
infuse the spirit of Christ into these spheres wherever
they have been perverted to selfishness ; and, next,
to include them within the recognised scope of the
Christian Church. It is unfortunately the case that
the name of the Christian Church has been appropriated almost exclusively to the organisation
for worship, instruction, and beneficence. But it is
impossible that this narrowing of the Divine purpose
should be permanent. We must endeavour to include
in our conception of the Church all the manifestations
of human excellence, and treat them as far as possible
as functions of the Church. Nor must we expect that
they will in every respect conform themselves to the
beliefs and practices of the organisation for worship
which is now almost exclusively called the Church.
They have their own sphere, in which they must act

B 2

freely. The demand that they should so conform themselves could only be rightly made if the Church organisation responded fully to the true ideal ; but this cannot be the case while the great spheres of the secular life are regarded as outside the Church organisation, and the leaders of them are not looked upon as ministers of Christ. The confusion which is thus created prevents the Church from using its full and Divine authority. It speaks with a hesitating and lisping utterance.

In the light of these remarks let us glance at the chief spheres and tendencies of the secular life.

1. Let us take the sphere of Science—that is, of the knowledge of the physical world which is chiefly in men's minds when they speak of science. Must we not admit that the discoveries which have been made in it have been to us real revelations or unveilings of God, and that their spiritual results have been of very great value ? The immutability of His will is shown in the reign of law, so that a lawless scepticism is rendered all but impossible. The true position of man is also made clear, so that a check is placed upon wilfulness and presumption. An end is put to mere speculation, and to systems like those of the schoolmen and some of the Encyclopædists of the last century, through the awe which is felt in the presence of the inevitable, the immense, and the irresistible. If some men of science are also rigid determinists (a result by no means necessary), they cannot be more so than Jonathan Edwards and Dr. Chalmers; and

if the tendency of the disclosure of the greatness of the physical world is to crush man, yet on the other hand a reaction and fresh uplifting comes to us from the spectacle which it presents of an eternal progress, from looking back on the long elaboration by which the dwelling of man has been prepared, and contemplating his history as one of constant rising from lower to higher stages.

There are indeed two difficulties which are apt to result from scientific studies; and which cause good men distress and perplexity ; but a solution of these seems near at hand. The revelations of science make us shrink from such breaches of the ordinary course of nature as seem to be involved in some of the Biblical histories, and to be intertwined with the historical sources of our faith. It would be impossible here to discuss the question thus opened. But a review of the long controversies which have taken place during the last 200 years on the subject, seems to lead us to these conclusions : first, that the main basis of Christian faith is not affected by it, since Christians have learnt to rest much more on the spiritual nature and power of Christ than on any special facts, even than on the testimony of His Resurrection ; and there are instances of men who hold earnestly to the name and spirit of Christ who yet do not admit any ·miraculous agency ;* and, secondly, that the Resurrection itself is to be viewed rather as a dis-

* See Dr. Abbott's " Through Nature to Christ."

closure of another state of existence* than as belonging to the order of events with which physical
science is conversant. There seems to be no reason
why our belief in an unchangeable order and our
hopes of immortality should disagree with one
another. The other danger connected with the life
of science is that it is so absorbing that the moral
world seems to disappear from the view. It has
even been said that the centre of interest is being
shifted from men to things. But we must view this
merely as a transitory phase. Men and women will
always be much more important than things, and
historical and moral studies will retain their pre-
eminence, even if they should suffer a temporary
eclipse. But, if the votaries of natural science are
almost exclusively absorbed in their own pursuit, we
should look upon this as the exercise of their special
Christian gift, the special mode in which they serve
God and men. It is hardly possible but that those
who have a special function, and are fulfilling it with
all their heart, should at times exaggerate its importance. But we cannot fail to observe that there is a
seriousness, a purity, and a disinterestedness about the
pursuits of natural science which give it a very high
moral value. If to Aristotle it seemed the most divine
of pursuits, it is quite possible that it may be a necessary antidote to the exclusive absorption in things moral
to which Christian seriousness has been apt to lean.

---

* Compare Bishop Horsley's "Four Sermons on the Resurrection,"
and Canon Westcott's "Gospel of the Resurrection."

2. We have to consider the life of Art, the pursuit of beauty and refinement, to which we may add the lighter pursuits—recreation and amusement. These must also be viewed as a mode in which one side of the Divine is made known to üs, and by which God is revealed and draws men to himself. It is sometimes said that art has nothing to do with religion. But it is in itself a part of religion. Without insisting on the fact that it often ministers powerfully to the moral and religious sentiments, or that the highest poetry and painting and sculpture and music is commonly the reflection of the best feelings of Christians and of citizens, we may reflect that art merely taken as a constituent of happiness is a revelation of one side of human and divine excellence. From the beginning it has been said that rest is a part of God's nature; and rest is precisely what art can give us. A life in which all art, all sense of beauty, all recreation, were suppressed, would be distinctly a lower life. And if there are times in which art has pre-eminently flourished, leaving a legacy of joy to future generations, so there are men who fulfil the same position for their contemporaries. We must not, indeed, yield to the false suggestion that such men are freed from moral restraints, or are not responsible for the use of their art. They are men, and man is, throughout the whole range of his energy, an accountable being. But we must not impose upon such men the terms which may justly apply to moralists and religious teachers.

3. But a few words need be said here in reference to the place of politics in our religious system. No one who reads St. Paul can doubt that the Christian doctrine is that God has established the government of nations, and that those who govern them are his ministers. In the wide sense which we have endeavoured to give to the Church, we need not scruple to speak of the nation as a branch of the Church. When we consider the vast interest which we have in the nation, and its vast power over us, when we reflect on the sacred duties of patriotism, and the other virtues which circle round it, we cannot but feel that there is nothing on earth nearer to God than the nation with which he has bound up our lives. If politics mean to us **a** care for the interests of the great brotherhood to which we belong, that is hardly distinguishable from the care for the kingdom of God : we can hardly be too much absorbed in it. The fault of Christian ministers is not that they care too much but too little for politics. We may rightly think of a statesman who directs uprightly the policy of England, involving as it does the welfare of all classes, the raising of the poor of the people, education, sanitation, temperance, thrift, justice, the maintenance of true relations between men and classes at home, a great and special power in European affairs, and the direct influence of Christian civilisation on barbarism, as in the fullest sense a minister of Christ and of God. And the sanctity which attaches to the supreme office ex-

tends in its measure to all subordinates in the political hierarchy, and to those who, directly or indirectly, contribute to their nomination. If the sacred church-functions of political life have at times been abused (as every church-function is apt to be) and have served the purposes of ambition and partisanship, the fault lies not alone with the individuals who are guilty of such perversion, but also with the false system which narrows the idea of the Church, and leaves outside its pale the duties of public life, which are the largest and among the noblest of its functions.

It is unnecessary to touch at any great length on the tendencies of the secular life in modern times which have been added to the enumeration of its three principal spheres—the tendencies of free criticism, democratic equality, and progress. But a few words may be said upon each. Criticism is merely the attempt to judge rightly. As such it is the result of the spirit of truth working in us. That it may, like other good things, be abused, being employed as the instrument of discontent or malevolence, or that it may degenerate into the mere habit of asking questions when we ought to be at work by the light of the truth which we possess, does not prevent our considering it as a necessary manifestation of the Christian spirit. We see its beneficial results on all sides, and positive truth stands out all the clearer for its operation. As to Democratic Equality, it is nothing else than the spirit of brotherhood demanding that those members of the community who have most to complain of should be in a position to get their grievances redressed. It does not imply that all have the same office, or that there is no difference between men in point of wealth, or social position, or culture, though it will constantly tend to reduce instead of increasing those inequalities. It is the expression under modern conditions of that demand for the care of the weak and helpless which in the politics of the Psalms and the Prophets of Israel was constantly pressed upon all who were in power. We need not hesitate to look upon the general movement which is often called the Revolution, and which has resulted in the substitution of constitutional government for autocracy almost all through Europe in the last thirty years as a great work of the Christian spirit. Lastly, the idea of progress is one which must be dear to every Christian, who believes that the present state of things is corrupt and full of selfishness, and who has learnt to pray, " Thy kingdom come." It is true that mere movement is not always progress ; but one who believes in the redemption of the world has an un-quenchable hope that it is being led on towards a goal grander than his best conceptions, but the out-lines of which stand out clearly before him ; and the . changes of recent times, if looked at in the spirit which has been suggested here, will seem to him in the main calculated to stimulate this hope.

But this view, it may be said, can only be accepted at the expense of large modifications in our theology.

The dogmas of the Church seem one by one to be challenged by these secular forces. Are we to yield to these? And where will the process of concession stop? It is quite true that theology must undergo some modifications; or, rather, it has undergone considerable modifications in our own time. Such questions as that of future punishment, the inspiration of Scripture, the Atonement, the Fatherhood of God, the state of the heathen, are almost universally treated in a different way from that in which they were treated even thirty years ago. The spirit in which they are dealt with is larger and more hopeful. And generally there is an unwillingness to use sharp dogmatic language, especially when it would imply a condemnation of some of the great secular tendencies which have here been dealt with. So far as this result is due to a recognition of these tendencies, we need not think it any derogation from Christianity or the Church to avow it, since these tendencies, as we have endeavoured to show, are themselves Christian tendencies; and we modify our convictions in obedience, not to a *force majeure* from without, but to the facts of Divine Providence and to the Christian spirit working in them. Nor need we fear the continuance of this process; in many respects its result will be to give more force to Christian doctrine. If the progress of scientific discovery makes us think of God less as a transcendent external power than as one immanent in the world, this is but giving a larger extension to the doctrine of the Spirit. If art and culture necessarily chasten the sharpness and the harshness of dogmatic teaching, and introduce us to a region where the direct interests of morality are not so obvious and exclusive, they will make the great objects of Christian thought loom out larger and more impressive, and the beauty of God and of holiness will take a wider expansion in our views. If political progress and the tendency to democratic equality demand the abolition of many restrictions, and the admission of lay or secular influences in departments of the Church hitherto controlled by the clergy, this is to be viewed as the drawing forth of new energy, an extension of the gifts of the Spirit. We need only demand that the process we are tracing should be conducted truthfully, and without rashness. Its result, we may be sure, will be not to limit or darken Christian teaching, but to give it the fuller expansion which, apart from the secular influences, it could never receive.

When Richard Rothe said that Christianity was the most mutable of all things, and that this was its special glory,* he did not imply any doubt of its essential principles, or any indifference to its form; he merely stated vividly its power of adaptation to changing circumstances, and its capacity for profiting by new discoveries of truth. Such a re-adaptation appears to be in progress now, and the object of the present publication is to help in effecting it. The

---

* Rothe's " Stille Stunden," p. 357, quoted in Hibbert Lectures for 1882, p. 294.

possible results of this re-adaptation are such as should fill every Christian with enthusiastic hope,'the hope of restoring unity where now there is division or mistrust, of extending the dominion of the Spirit of Christ, of combining elements which now neutralise each other in the task of elevating the whole life of mankind ; for in that direction lies the Kingdom of God.

The scope of the sermons will be seen from the following epitome :—

1. Christian faith is not an adherence to a series of propositions, but a living sympathy and aspiration, which shows itself in many forms, and is the spring of a true and healthful life.

2. The Church is not chiefly a system of public worship designed to direct men's minds to another world, but a social state in which the Spirit of Christ reigns; and this state appears in many ways both within and without the recognised field of the Church's energy.

3. The Spirit of Christ is supreme over the whole range of the secular life, education, trade, literature art, science, and politics, and is seen to be practically vindicating this supremacy.

4. The peculiar privilege which the Church claims for itself and its members is not that of exclusive rights, but of leadership in a work to which all are

called ; and, as such, it is in accordance with the natural order, and with a true universalism.

5. Criticism is not a foe, but a friend, to Christian teaching and piety.

6. Each individual who has the Spirit of Christ is to be recognised in his own sphere as exercising a function or ministry of the Church, according to the doctrine of the universal priesthood of believers.

7. The theological doctrine on which this depends is the immanence of God—"God is a Spirit."

8. Intellectual pursuits are harmonised by Christianity, considered as a life.

9. The doctrine of progress, so fully recognised in the spheres of industry and science, is also applicable to theology, which must open itself out to new influences, and appropriate them.

I.

Unity through a Moral Faith.

I.

Unity through a Moral Faith.

(Preached before the University of Oxford, November 24, 1878.)

" He is our peace, who hath made both one and hath broken down the wall of partition between us, having abolished in His flesh the enmity, even the law of commandments contained in ordinances, for to make in Himself of twain one new man, so making peace."— EPHESIANS ii. 14, 15.

THE fact which St. Paul describes in these striking words was to him the centre and marrow of Christianity. Christ is the great reconciler. In Him God and man meet together. In Him all the creation is to be gathered into one. In Him all parts of the human family, which before were separated, flow together and are at peace.

The subsequent career of Christianity cannot be said to be altogether of a piece with this experience and these hopes of the Apostle. It must appear to every observer that Christianity has very frequently been, by its internal discord, and by its harsh bearing towards mankind, the promoter of strife, not of peace. It is clear, therefore, to every believer that there is some foreign element which has been joined with it, and which thus mars in its later career the purpose so largely fulfilled in its first beginnings.

C

We must seek to eliminate the foreign element by drawing out and expanding the central truth, and by promoting in men that attitude towards Christ and one another which originally made faith a humanising principle.

Let us first notice how vast a range of thought is included in St. Paul's assertion that all are made one in Christ. It is hardly too much to say that this was to St. Paul the Gospel itself, the good news of God's universal love. His first knowledge of Christianity as a working power had probably been gained from the preaching of Stephen, which plainly intimated that religion was not bound up with the local peculiarities of Judaism. And what he knew of Christ himself must have been in conformity with this. The extraordinary feature to the Jewish mind in our Lord's life and teaching was its universality. There is nothing in it which is merely Judaic. It is not exclusively of any nation or tongue, but belongs alike to all. This was what sharpened the enmity of the Jewish rulers against Him, and was the real cause of His death. The Pharisaism which had become the religion of the Jews was exclusive; and the attitude of Christ towards the Publicans and other outcast classes, who symbolised to the orthodox Jews the whole outside world, jarred upon the pride of the dominant belief. Men felt that, if this doctrine succeeded, their superiority was gone; and therefore they revolted from it.

The young man brought up at the feet of Gamaliel had shared to the fullest extent this Judaic exclusiveness; and, when Stephen accentuated the universality of Christianity, Saul became a persecutor. But this very characteristic which made him hate and destroy the Christian faith became eventually the thing most precious to him. It haunted him, we cannot doubt, in his journey to Damascus; and it was the point on which his conversion turned. The Jesus who appeared to him in the way was the universal Saviour; and the apostolate which he received was that of the Gentiles. This universality was the point for which he contended at the Council at Jerusalem and in his opposition to Peter at Antioch. This was the special object of the attacks of the Judaizers upon him. The recognition of this universality was the object which he sought in going to Jerusalem with the offerings of the Gentiles. This excited the hatred of the Jews against him, and this was the cause of his imprisonment and his death.

It was not a doctrine merely but a fact. The Jews turned away from the universality of the Gospel but the Gentiles and the remnant embraced it; and it became the standing marvel which the infant churches presented to mankind. St. Paul is never weary of repeating how Jew and Gentile, barbarian and Greek, slave and freeman, had all felt a new power of cohesion and became as brothers, members of one family, enjoying equal rights, greeting one another with the kiss of charity. This was the real power, the power of social affection, the new-born enthusiasm of humanity of which Christ was the source. And it was felt like the attraction which draws lovers together. The great deeps of human nature were broken up; the power of love overflowed its ancient boundaries; and men in whom difference of race and of custom had begotten an alienation which seemed like a law of nature, fell into each other's arms and were at peace. They knelt at the same devotions, the Sacrament was their common meal; that which divided them had disappeared, and a new life, unfettered by the peculiarities which had before bred enmity, was forming itself in their young societies.

This view of religious truth is developed to some extent in the earlier epistle of St. Paul. It is essential to the right understanding of the epistles to the Romans and Galatians, in which the characteristic so dear to St. Paul is expressed by the central term Faith, while the Judaic pride which caused division lurks in "the Law;" and in which the Apostle constantly breaks out into expressions like these: "Is he the God of the Jews only? Is he not of the Gentiles also? Seeing it is one God who shall justify the circumcision by faith and the uncircumcision through faith." But it is in the later epistles that it assumes its most marked pre-eminence. St. Paul speaks of it as an experience, an acquisition. The Churches have realised it: the Apostle's great conviction has been lived out and has taken shape in actual society. It is now the mystery which he had been specially called to preach, but which had lain hid for ages and genera-

tions till it was manifested in Christ.   This enables
St. Paul to look out over the field of the opening
Christian history, and to announce that God's purpose
is to gather all things into one in Christ.   The harmony which he feels within him, and which he sees
reigning among his converts, is projected upon the
development of the world itself; and the reconciling
power of Christ brings all men and all things into
one.

When we compare this magnificent prospect with
the result of eighteen centuries, we thankfully acknowledge that, in part at least, it has been fulfilled.   The
sense of harmony in the creation generally, and between its higher and lower parts, has increased to a
conviction of unity which is the basis of all inquiry,
of all science, of all practical progress.   The sense
of brotherhood in the human race has asserted itself.
Slavery is all but done away with, wars are conducted
with an underlying sense of unity: the civilised nations are bound together by a community of arts, of
knowledge, of literature, by certain acknowledged
principles of justice, by some similarity of institutions, by some consensus, however feeble, of religious
faith.   But how slowly have these come about.   How
imperfect are they at the best.   And how many antagonisms remain unsubdued, and even seem at times
to grow fiercer and more irreconcilable.   And how
often has the progress, such as it has been, towards
unity, been won, not by the proclamation of Christian
truth through its recognised channels, but in oppo-

sition to them and by other means; so that many begin to doubt whether Christianity has not lost its virtue, and, in the struggle which is stirred up by a Church which has parted with its healing power, are tempted to side with its professed antagonists.

We cannot deny that Christianity often appears as a fosterer not of unity but of division ; and the excuse for this which is sometimes sought in the words of our Lord which speak of his sending not peace but the sword is quite inapplicable. For Christ's enmity was against evil alone : but we have connected with evil, things which are really indifferent ; and we war against these as if they were evil in themselves. We do what was done by the heathen, or by the Jews in the time of their decadence, we erect our own peculiarities into good and debase those of others into evil ; and thus we fill the world with our enmities, and connect them with Christ, whose name we thus take in vain and whose cause we expose to contempt. The work of the Christian teacher is to isolate from this false conflict the good and the evil, so that men may see where the issue really lies, and may take their side undoubtingly. Our way through life is thickly beset with contradictions which owe their origin to misconceptions of Christianity. There is the conflict of Papist and Protestant, that of Churchman and Dissenter in England, that of various parties within our own religious organisation, that of clerical and lay interests in matters of education, of marriage, of charities, of the provision for religious worship: there is the conflict, to use the popular language, between science and revelation, and again, between religion and culture: and, beyond all these, perhaps the greatest antagonism of all, that between spirituality and common life. Can it be pretended that any of these is in itself the battle of faith, the conflict which Christ predicted? Can we say that the cause which we ourselves espouse in any of these conflicts is absolutely good and its opposite absolutely evil? Can it be maintained that those who are supposed to represent the right and the Christian side are so managing the conflict as to war against evil alone? Or is it not rather true that Christian things are often aimed at in an unchristian way, and Christian opinion upheld by unchristian methods; and that he who tries to judge truth fully must often stand in doubt on which side the truth really lies, nay, sometimes perceive that truth has passed over from the so-called Christian camp to that of its opponents; and that, while men on one side are saying, Lord, Lord, it is on the other that the things are done which Christ said.

And the consequence of this habit of making antagonisms instead of removing them is that those who stand in doubt have their doubts confirmed, or turn away from the whole scene in which such antagonisms arise. It has become quite natural for men to hear it said that a thing is Christian *and yet* tolerant, or peaceful, or liberal; or even to hear that a thing is

Christian and therefore intolerant, illiberal, and the cause of constant strife. And so some who might be attracted by a religion of love are tempted "to shun the dreary, uncouth place," and to seek their rest elsewhere. I suppose we have all known men who, from the Babel of mutual condemnations with which the Church is filled, have quietly, and not quite unreasonably, resolved to think no more upon religious subjects. And that which is done deliberately by a few is done unconsciously by a vast multitude. Love is attractive, but strife is repulsive to mankind. And those who thus turn away to find spiritual rest elsewhere are not wholly doing wrong nor are they always disappointed. The spirit which amidst the waves of controversy finds no rest for the sole of its foot, flies naturally to harbour on some shore which, however rugged, is at least free from discord.

We have to set forth Christianity once more as the great reconciling power. We cannot allow it to be identified with dissension. It must not be dishonoured in the present generation of its ministers by proving in their hands inadequate to the task of bringing all the varieties of human life and of human nature into harmony. Whatever diversities are occasioned by genuine conviction are to be treated as St. Paul treated the various gifts of the Church in his day. There are diversities of gifts but the same Spirit. There are differences of character, of opinion, of organisation, different points of view, different modes of life, differences of education and of reading ;

but there is one divine power which works through them all unless they be selfish or insincere, and draws them all into harmony. To trace out that power, to bring it into relief, to eliminate from it the sources of discord, is one of the most fruitful tasks which a Christian preacher can set before himself and those who hear him.

In order to do this, we need not go to any other quarter than the grand doctrine of St. Paul which is affirmed by our own Church with special emphasis, the doctrine of salvation through faith only : the doctrine that faith is the supreme, the central, the all-sufficing principle, in comparison with which all else is insignificant, the token of standing or falling in the Church or in the individual. We have only to rally men once more to this great battle cry of the spiritual warfare, showing what it means to the thought of the present day, pointing out how grand and simple a thing faith is, and eliminating from it all that is not essential. If we can do this and can show where in the present day the chief fields for its exercise lie, we may do something towards abolishing our angry differences, by helping men to rise above them.

The central object of faith is God as He is revealed in Jesus Christ. The image of Christ, the ideal of His life, this it is which declares and makes known to us what God really is ; and this, presented to the mind and embraced by faith, has power to bring all men into unity. We have been far too apt to look at this as if it were an object for precise intellectual statement ; and then faith has become a matter of minute knowledge, instead of being a grand and simple affection in which all our powers are combined. What we need is to realise that faith is a deep moral principle, which, because it is so simple, shows itself in a thousand different ways, in the child and in the man, in the untaught and in the learned, in those in whom faith is beginning and those in whom it has reached a full development. We need to get rid of its limitations, and to make all men in whom it is working realise that it is theirs ; to recognise it wherever it is found, to trace it in its direct forms, and to draw the whole world within its all-embracing unity.

1. Faith is trust in a person. But we are not to exact that he in whom it exists should have satisfied himself minutely as to every part of the object towards which his faith is directed, for that object is moral and infinite. In the present day it is impossible for us to have an absolute historical certainty about many of the events in the life of our Lord out of which grows that image which we recognise as divine. This does not imply that the moral image is blurred, or that the main outlines of the character are objects of doubt. The existence of the Church, the Christian character throughout its history, the self-consistency of the ideal presented in the Gospel, the far-reaching truths which encircle it, the complete originality of the life and words which yet ally themselves with human nature in all ages and climes, are

so many anchors of our faith which make it certain
that there is a fitting and adequate object to which
it is directed. But faith is a spiritual, not an intellectual act. It cannot, indeed, live if its supposed
object is non-existent, and it is ruined by a false
profession. Nevertheless, it is not so tied to facts
and definitions that it must halt and hesitate till
every question which can be asked concerning the
nature of God and the life of Christ is fully answered.
It is much more important that faith should be
sincere than that it should be fully informed. Faith
is akin to love, and love is often genuine when its
object is dimly seen. Nay, since we acknowledge
the Godhead to be immense and incomprehensible,
it is quite possible that the most genuine faith should
be that of a child's simplicity and ignorance, rather
than that of a man's reasoning intellect; and, as a
fact of Christian history, faith has suffered much
more from over-definition than from indistinctness in
its object. Certainly the greatest quarrels among
Christians have arisen from the attempt to define
what might well have been left indefinite, what truthfulness would have declared it impossible to define.
Let it be enough for us that we have in the Gospels
an image of goodness which represents to us the
character of God. To that our faith adheres, and
finds in it life and peace.

2. But, further, the faith which unites us to the
image of Christ is deeper as well as less definite than
it is commonly assumed by theologians to be. It is

not a mere assent, but a living sympathy with goodness.   That which made the disciples exclaim, " Thou
art the Christ, the Son of the living God," or, " Lord,
show us the Father, and it sufficeth us," was not that
part of His life which is strange and unintelligible to
us, or which historical criticism may tend to make
uncertain, but that which we can share with Him,
that which draws out the sympathy of our common
nature.   It was the love, the truthfulness, the forbearance, the tenderness, the resolute self-sacrifice which
their master displayed, and which was drawn forth
more distinctly when trials deepened and the shades
thickened round Him in the closing months of His
ministry.   Of this image mankind can never be
robbed.   However men may differ as to the precise
events in which this image of goodness was manifested, the character which is expressed in the two
constantly-recurring words of St. Paul, " The love of
Christ," and " The cross of Christ," will always remain
to mankind as the highest expression of moral goodness, as the divine manifested in human nature.

To this it is that faith attaches itself.   We are
conscious as we look upon the image of Christ, that
we have at least the capacity for feelings and deeds
like His.   If the first result of the view of a supreme
goodness is that which finds vent in the words
" Depart from me, for I am a sinful man, O Lord,"
yet there is really generated in us a sympathy with
the goodness which seems so distant from us.   We
own it in our consciences as that which is best, as

that which ought to be ours. It lights up for us the whole moral world, it brings out good and evil in their most marked colours ; and it discloses to us the true character of moral goodness, freeing it from the integuments with which selfishness had bound it up. We know, by that conscience which is the reflection of the divine truth within us, and which the image of Christ tends constantly to purge from its natural dimness, that this is what the supreme mind must approve, that this is the image of the invisible God.

And the sympathy which we thus feel is independent of particular systems. The metaphysical questions even as to the nature of God do not affect it vitally. Whether the strict monotheistic tendency be maintained, or whether that more spiritual tendency prevail which tends to trace out the divine in the evolving forces of nature and of mankind, the image of Christ remains ever before us, chastening our speculations, and bringing us back to human life as the proper study of mankind, and making us feel that, since man is the head of the creation, and the image of God, the true entrance to theology and religion is not in metaphysics but in morals, not in speculation as to the origin of matter or the natural history of the world, but in a right estimate of moral goodness, and a heart-felt sympathy with it. It is the heart that makes the Christian ; and the heart is occupied, not with the subtilties and disputation of metaphysics, but with the reconciling power of love.

Moreover, the more we believe in a Christ who is

the divine type, the root, the holder together of all
the creation and of all human nature, the more
certain we feel that, in holding to truth and love
where they are found, men are holding to Christ
himself. By unbelievers this might be doubted ; but
by believers in Christ it must be held true. And this
enables us to embrace (whether they respond to the
embrace or not) all who have a sympathy with goodness, even in its simplest elements. They may
misconceive of the metaphysical nature of God, or
the relation of the Father to the Son ; they may not
be able to receive some of the facts relating to the life
of Christ as told us in the Gospel ; nay, it may be
that through prejudice they may deem it right to
combat many things which Christians hold dear, to
rank themselves and be ranked by us among unbelievers, and yet there may be in them still a real and
deep faith, a faith far truer than that which blindly
assents to all the articles of our Churches ; and the
object of this faith, dimly seen or misconceived as
it may be by them, is none other than the image of
Christ, which is made to appear to them, not full-
orbed in the splendour and force of His personality,
but diffused through literature, and art, and history,
and politics, and philanthropy, and the whole human
society, which, once possessed of Him, can never
again forget Him. The faith which is strongest, and
which unites men together is not primarily the belief
in the Church or the sacraments, in the miraculous
birth of Christ or his bodily resurrection, nor even

that which we call, perhaps with too much confidence and strictness, the Personality of God. These are the supports and guarantees, the external fences or the outgrowths of faith. But the faith which saves and which makes us true to our Lord is that which welcomes truth and goodness, and treasures them up; for these are the very nature of God. Let the heart be filled with the image of Christ; and this will lead you on to life and immortality, to a fuller view of God, and to the filling up of the outlines of the life of Christ. But the reverse process does not necessarily hold good. Doctrines and facts are no substitutes for faith, nor even the necessary channels through which it courses. It was not the highest faith which dictated the cry, "Blessed is the womb that bare thee and the paps which thou hast sucked." "Yea rather," says Christ, "blessed are they which hear the Word of God and keep it."

3. Faith is not only trust and sympathy but aspiration. This makes it at once both deeper and wider in its embrace; deeper, because it involves a personal appropriation of that divine goodness which is the object of faith; wider, because it recognises as partakers of faith all who, from whatever distance, are tending and aspiring towards the same spiritual centre. It is a commonplace among divines and preachers that a very imperfect knowledge is consistent with true faith, and that a very little faith will save a man. And every one who is conversant with the deeper feelings of men must have observed

how often amidst their apparent carelessness there emerges a longing for good, a discontent with their present condition, a longing for some ideal, dimly seen, but which the heart confesses and appropriates. Such an aspiration, such a faith, may be found in the wayward longings of the heathen, "Seeking the Lord if haply they may feel after Him and find Him." It may be found in the silent faith of men "Perplexed in faith but pure in deed." It may be found in many of the strange and formal expressions of those whose form of belief repels us, but who sincerely follow the truth as they understand it. We need never doubt that, as the fuller truth appears to them, they will embrace it, and we must strive to bring that fuller truth before them. But meanwhile we can acknowledge each honest desire for good as the witness of the presence of genuine faith. It is not the part of Christians to deny or make light of such an aspiration whenever it may be found, but to assume it to be the mark of the drawing of the Divine Spirit, and by their sympathy to foster it into maturity.

This faith, which we have thus tried to illustrate in its simplest elements of trust, of sympathy, of aspiration, St. Paul announced as a power which liberated men from "the law of commandments contained in ordinances." Those formal injunctions, decrees, or *dogmas* (so the word stands in the Greek) which have been taken to be the permanent expressions of the Divine whether among the Jews or among the heathen, were swept away by the breath of faith. Not that they were necessarily abrogated as human institutions, but that the human spirit, even while obeying them, felt itself free, by soaring above them into the higher atmosphere of faith and love. Judaism had been a powerful means (as it is even now) of binding men together. But its bond was that of a sectional union, which had become antagonistic to the fuller union demanded by Christian universality. It was a shield on one side of which was inscribed " Union of the chosen people," but on the other, " Alienation from all mankind." And, cost what it might, the Apostle proclaimed the abolition of the Jewish ordinances or dogmata—their abolition, that is, as a binding and divine sanction for society. Christian faith and love was henceforth to be the only and all-sufficient bond of union. What! are we to trust to a mere attachment to a person, a fleeting, unstable sentiment, instead of the grand old institutions of the law, which have been like the firmament above us and the solid ground beneath our feet? How weak! How infatuated! How contrary to all experience! How lawless! How ignorant of our poor human nature, which needs these dogmata for its support! Such must have been the cries of Pharisees and of worldly men alike ; for to such men the devices and management of clever persons, and the *pondus inertiæ* of the lower elements of human life are always the basis of calculation. But faith and love were stronger bonds than Jewish or Gentile ordinances, and the spiritual law was more binding

D

than the external law. And whenever Christian preachers have dared to trust themselves, like St. Paul, to the simple force of conviction and love, they have reaped a harvest which no support of ordinances and dogmas could ever bring them.

Are we not suffering, my brethren, in the present day from the bondage of the ordinances or dogmas of the past? Are not these precisely the things which need to be " taken out of the way," if Christianity is to be once more a reconciler, not a divider? The controversies of the 16th and .17th centuries were hardened down into institutions of worship and propositions about Christian doctrine which, in their rigid, unbending form, have become the perpetuators of separation. They do not, when taken as absolute and exclusive formularies, correspond to the convictions of the present day, and they are, as such, quite alien from the more spiritual life which our age demands. It is not that these institutions or dogmata require any revolutionary handling, any more than St. Paul would have wished to destroy the social and political customs of the Jews ; what is needed is such an adaptation of Christian worship as will recognise the requirements of all true worshippers, and such an explanation of dogmas as will allow room for the larger convictions which are the necessary growth of the three most active centuries of the world and the Church's history. But just as St. Paul dethroned the law from its exclusive supremacy and its supposed everlasting sanction which had made it the foe of faith, so must the Christian preacher of our day fight against the tendency which he sees on all sides to erect the ordinances of the 4th century or the 8th, of the 16th or the 17th, into everlasting barriers. Not circumcision nor uncircumcision—not Catholic nor Protestant, not Church or Dissent, not Episcopacy or other forms of Church government, nor the articles and theological statements of Nice or Rimini or Toledo, not the decrees of the Council of Trent or the Augsburg Confession, or the XXXIX. Articles, or the Westminster Catechism, but faith that worketh by love, and the keeping of the commandments of God.

I had hoped to touch upon another portion of this subject, and to show that faith must be recog nised in the present day as developing itself in the common relations of life quite as much as in worship or in preaching; and that a due attention to this is one of the most hopeful means of furthering union amongst men. But the time fails me. I may hope to address you at a future time on this and similar points. For the present let me urge upon the various sections of opinion how the supremacy of Christian faith, when fully acknowledged, may help them to be at one and to promote that godliness and honesty for which unity is so greatly required.

Is it too much to assume that the ideal of the Christian life is common to us all, acknowledged by us all as morally supreme? It seems to me, at least, that it has never been seriously questioned; for those

who attack Christian systems rarely, if ever, attack
the ideal of the Christian life; nay, such men are
frequently the most vehement assertors of truly Christian principles, and not rarely appeal to Christian
sanctions for their enforcement.   Does any one really
doubt that the life of self-devotion and love, of truth
and courage, which is the Christian ideal, is the true
life of man ?   Or, again, that this ideal is itself "the
truth," the central and paramount truth to which all
other kinds of truth are secondary.

   1. Are there, then, some among us who, by their
excessive value for Christian ordinances or dogmas,
for sacraments, and the order of the ministry, are
practically placing the life of Christian faith in the
second rank ?   Let them consider whether, in their
zeal for those things which they account the fences
and bulwarks of Christianity, they are not letting the
essence escape them.   It has been said that the
Roman Catholic system is a vast apparatus for
guarantees, under which the thing guaranteed is apt
to disappear.   And the same thing may be said of
that tendency which may be called Clericalism, which
is dominant in the Anglican Church at the present
day.   No one can fail to see that this tendency is
alienating class after class of men.   Where it reigns
unchecked, all elements of free thought are repressed,
lest some dogma should be shaken; no form of
Protestantism except the Anglican Church is recognised, and yet we are no nearer to union with any of
the forms of so-called Catholicism, the three chief

sections of which cannot kneel together at the sacrament. And, further, religion is being gradually
eliminated from common life, and is thought of as
consisting only in services, and preaching, and devotional practices ; and hence the breach between the
Church and the world grows wider. And, wherever
this is the case, the Christian ideal suffers. Elements
of good which thrive in the open atmosphere of the
common life of mankind are disowned ; and the great
Christian ideal is drawn down from its commanding
position of universality to become the life of the
cloister or the confessional, of the clique or the
coterie, timorous instead of manly, narrow instead of
expansive, suspicious of change and of discovery, the
foe of human progress instead of its most ardent
promoter. It is supposed, no doubt, that, although
the witness of experience is such as I have just
described, yet there is an obligation on us to obey
certain injunctions of discipline or of doctrine which
are presumed to have a divine authority, and to
uphold them in their most rigid form, whatever the
consequences may be. But the doctrine of the
supremacy of faith places these injunctions in their
true position. They are in any case of secondary,
not primary, importance. If we can but acknowledge that all these ordinances or dogmas are only of
virtue as conducing to the Christian life, and that this
Christian life and the fellowship which flows from it
is the first thing, to which all else must be subordinate, the evils which I have noticed as flowing from

clericalism would soon be counteracted. What is called for is not so much the abandonment of particular practices or dogmas, as that these practices or dogmas should be viewed as holding the second rank, as comparatively indifferent, that they should be modified by the experience of their effect upon the life of individuals and of the community, that facts as to piety and conduct lying outside the range of our own peculiar system should not only not be ignored, but be sought out and compared, that the unity of the spirit should be supreme, and the unity of external order be secondary.

2. And are there some, again, who, repelled by the dogmatism and narrowness which has been admitted into Christian systems, are tempted to put the whole matter aside? Since you find Christianity identified by many of its teachers with a system which seems to deny freedom and progress and to assert as essential what is really questionable, are you induced to doubt whether it is possible honestly to remain Christians at all? It is surely worth while to ask whether you are not giving too great weight to assertions which have no necessary authority, however widely they may be received, and whether you are not mistaking for the essence what is really the accident. If the Christian ideal is unimpeachable, and if the ideal of life is really the thing of central importance, then the fact that a system of institutions or dogmas has grown up around it which is of doubtful or less than doubtful good, must not be

allowed to make us indifferent to the best gift of God to us. I believe that there are many who, with generous dispositions and a wish to do good, are repelled from all the ordinary forms of Christian activity by the association of these with a Church system full of assumptions with which they cannot agree. We cannot pronounce your shibboleths, they say, and, therefore, we cannot join with you ; but is it right, I ask, to shut up our sympathies because there is some dogmatic hardness in others ? In some matters of a voluntary kind such a course no doubt is justifiable. Some society which we are asked to join has its management distracted by petty controversy, and we may rightly refuse to join it and may carry our energies elsewhere. But you cannot do this with the all-embracing society of the Christian Church. The effort to do moral work outside of it or without and reference to it can hardly ever produce more than sectional and transient results ; for it implies that we leave out of view the greatest of all the features of the common interest. You may begin some good work without any reference to Christianity ; but sooner or later you come in contact with Christian belief and Christian institutions. It may be, of course, that the perplexity is so hopeless that you must stand outside and live your life apart, and leave to a future generation the task of harmonising what you do with the general good. There are many such lives lived now, and it is not for the Church to disown them. But I urge upon those who are so living to

ask themselves whether there is any valid reason for
their isolation.   Is not the desire for good and the
zeal which you feel within you truly Christian, and
the very essence of Christianity?   Can you, and can
those who follow you, afford to dispense with the
help of the great Christian brotherhood?   And have
you any right to leave to those who come after you a
tangled web to unweave, and an occasion of fresh
misunderstanding?   Is it not a manlier thing to face
the larger problems instead of being content with
merely sectional action?   If the Christian doctrine is
cumbrous and allied to some things which are false,
show by your life, and by any contributions you can
make to the solution of our difficulties, the power of
a simpler faith.   If the Church is overlaid with things
non-essential, take your part in reforming it on a
better model.   But do not give up the grandest of all
objects to which the mind of man can apply itself, the
building up of the great temple of humanity in har-
monious conviction and united energy beneath the
broad canopy which the Christian ideal has raised to
shelter all mankind.

3. Once more, are there some of us who are
accustomed to speak of the supremacy of faith, and
who would echo the words of the Reformer that this
is the article of a standing or a falling Church, but
who hold what may be called a traditional view of
what faith means and what it does?   Are there some
to whom faith means a belief in certain propositions,
and justification merely a sentence of acquittal, and

the manner in which justification has been brought
about a compact by which it is arranged that the
innocent should endure a penalty instead of the
guilty? I have no doubt that true faith is constantly
to be found under the disguise (for so it must be
called) of statements such as these, which are a
hardening down into logical form of the deep and
passionate expressions of divine rhetoric or poetry.
But I would make two requests of those who cast
their faith in such moulds as these: 1st, That they
would not exact these shibboleths from all whom
they teach, nor judge others who cannot pronounce
them to be unbelievers, nor do themselves and the
Church the wrong of isolating themselves into a
party; but that they would try to trust others and
would open themselves to free discussions which will
rob them, let them be well assured, of nothing which
is essential, but will give wider scope to their sympathies and greater reality to a well-tested faith; and
2ndly, I would urge them to hold fast ·by their own
principle of the supremacy of faith and not to fall
back into a feeble ecclesiasticism. Those who revived
among us the doctrines of justification by faith and
conversion of life in the beginning of this century
did not appeal to the order of the ministry or the
special and exclusive customs of our Church, but
set men face to face with God and the Christian
life: and if their doctrine is to be developed by
their spiritual heirs, it must be not by adding to
it conditions which mar its very essence, but by

making it more divinely simple and more divinely comprehensive.

4. Can we not, my brethren, unite all lovers of good, all to whom the image of Christ is dear, in one great sustained effort against evil, the only real foe? Why should there be parties any more? Why cannot we all be one party, the party of good against evil?

St. Paul says that the power by which Christ conquered the dogmas of his day was the cross. "He took them out of the way, nailing them to his cross." The self-renunciation for the sake of universal love of which the cross is the complete expression was the destruction of the proud isolation of the dogmatic system. And that is the power by which alone we can get rid of the party-making dogmas of our time. We must stoop and we must suffer, that we may be at peace. Peace is not to be won by easily and weakly yielding to those tendencies of our day which would establish a religion of selfishness, but by that humility which is willing to put aside its own conceit and to confess itself a fool that it may be spiritually wise : which accepts and glories in that which is simplest and humblest in religion. It seems at times as if men were almost unconsciously coming round to this simpler faith. I have often been surprised to find among those who have in public contended most eagerly and harshly for their favourite dogmas a very simple and homely Christian standard accepted in their private relations. Beneath those things which divide us it is not hard to perceive a general acquiescence in that Christian ideal in which we are at one. The image of our Lord is really at the root of our religion. Let us be content with this, and hold all other things subordinate to it ; and we shall attract all true hearts to our side and war heartily and without vacillation against selfishness in all its forms.

And you, young men, who are preparing here for the conflicts of the world, and by the free life and thought of the University are strengthening your wills and setting the edge of your moral dispositions and forming your opinions for your future career ; I beg you, do not cast away the freedom which you enjoy by addicting yourselves slavishly to any of the special systems between which young minds are apt to oscillate and in which older minds get unhappily fixed. Lay a firm grasp by faith on that image of goodness which is held out to you in Jesus Christ. Seek to appropriate that goodness by prayer and aspiration ; acknowledge it frankly wherever it is to be found in others ; try to bring within the range of its influence every part of your life, your study, your amusements, your social intercourse, your intellectual conflicts ; ask yourself, in reference to any plan or proposition, not whether it is pleasant, nor whether it will square with certain preconceived opinions of your own or of others, but whether it is right and true. And when you have got sight of truth and goodness, work steadily towards it till it is obtained. Then you will constantly minister to the cause of Christian goodness, of love, of unity ; and in your future calling, whatever it may be, you will exercise upon those about you that attractive and redemptive influence which will ever accompany those who have within them the image of Christ.

II.

Religion without a Temple.

Religion without a Temple.

(Preached before the University of Oxford, February 2nd, 1879.)

"And I saw no temple therein : for the Lord God Almighty and the Lamb are the temple of it. And the city had no need of the sun, neither of the moon, to shine in it : for the glory of God did lighten it, and the Lamb is the light thereof. And the nations of them which are saved shall walk in the light of it : and the kings of the earth do bring their glory and honour into it."—REVELATIONS xxi. 22—24.

THE secret which the Apocalypse, in common with all prophecy, has disclosed to this generation, shows us that the seer was representing, for the comfort of his contemporaries, the times, not far off, but near at hand, the things which he says must shortly come to pass—the hour that cometh, and now is. The principles which are enunciated apply to all times, but the vivid descriptions which are drawn apply primarily to the events which are beginning to dawn on the spiritual insight of the prophet. The new Jerusalem is not the description solely, if chiefly, of the state to which Christians may look forward beyond the grave ; it is primarily the description of Christendom, the actual Christian society, idealised, no doubt, but intended in all its chief spiritual features to find its realisation now and here. It presents to us an ideal towards which we are to strive, as one capable of attainment ; and, while the spiritual and the critical faculty alike reject the piecing together of the ideal picture with its antitype, they alike teach us that here, as with all earnest poetry, reality lies at the base of the metaphor. John meant that the Church which he longed for should be what his imagery foreshadows.

The feature in this ideal to which the text gives prominence is, when we consider it, nothing less than astounding; namely, this—that the appliances of worship are completely absent. This seer of the primitive Church was, as the whole book shows, Jewish to the backbone. He wrote, as criticism tends to show, just at the time when the Roman eagles were about to swoop down upon Jerusalem, the Holy City. That city was identified with the temple which was its centre. The capital and the point of union of the Jewish nation was a place of worship. Yet in St. John's ideal of the new Jerusalem, which was in many things to be the counterpart of the old, these words stand forth in all their naked grandeur, " I saw no temple therein !" And if these words imply, as they unquestionably do, that the ideal of the primitive Church was one, not of worship, but of a life pervaded by the Spirit of God : if we accept, as we are bound to do, this ideal as our own, then we must admit that the history of the Church presents something which is even more astounding —namely this, that the Church has looked upon public worship and its appliances as its main object and function. During the whole of the Middle Ages, that first great effort at the realisation of the Christian ideal, the building of places of worship, and the organising of hierarchies to serve them, was almost the sole thought of Christians; so that the Reformation had to set about the melancholy work of pulling down the splendid abbeys and chantries, the fruit of a misdirected zeal. Their doom was shadowed forth in the words of William Tyndale, the translator of the Scriptures, and one of the most far-seeing of our Reformers, in the answer he gave to the jest of Sir Thomas More about the building of Tenterden steeple. The great Chancellor's jest is widely known ; the Reformer's answer deserves to be known as widely : "Neither intend I to prove to you that Paul's steeple is the cause why the Thames is broke in about Erith, or that Tenterden steeple is the cause of the decay of Sandwich Haven, as Master More jesteth. Nevertheless, this I would were persuaded unto you (as it is true), that the building of them and such like, through the false faith that we have in them, is the decay of all the havens in England, and of all the cities, towns, highways, and shortly of the whole commonwealth. For since these false monsters crope up into our conciences, and robbed us of the knowledge of our Saviour Jesus Christ, making us believe in such popeholy works, and to think that there was none other way into Heaven, we have not wearied to build them

E

abbeys, cloisters, colleges, chauntries, and cathedral churches with high steeples, striving and envying one another who should do most. And as for the deeds which pertain to our neighbours and to the common-wealth, we have not regarded at all, as things which seem no holy works, or such as God would not once look upon. And, therefore, we left them unseen to, until they were past remedy, or past our power to remedy them; inasmuch as our slow bellies, with their false blessings, had juggled away from us that wherewith they might have been holpen in due season. So that the silly poor man (though he had haply no wisdom to ex-press his mind, or that he durst not, or that Master More fashioneth his tale, as he doth other men's, to jest out the truth) saw that neither Goodwin Sands, nor any other cause alleged, was the decay of Sandwich Haven, so much as that the people had no heart to maintain the commonwealth, for blind devotion which they had to pope-holy works." (*Demaus' Life of Tyndale*, p. 277.)

That Tyndale should have had to write this 1,500 years after the vision of Patmos is strange enough. But if it is strange that the Church of the darker ages should have needed so bitter a lesson, is it not ten times stranger still that the Church of the days of greater enlightenment should be found again making the chief part of its business the organising of the modes of worship, that the largest efforts which are owned as the efforts of the Church are made for the establishment and maintenance of worship — that our chief controversies relate to the teaching and the ministry of a system designed primarily, if not exclusively, for worship—that even the fancies and the refinements of such a system divide us—that the breach between things secular and things religious grows wider instead of their being made to blend into one—and that the vast and fruitful spaces of the actual life of mankind lie still so largely without the gates? The old Jerusalem was all temple. The mediæval Church was all temple. But the ideal of the new Jerusalem was—no temple, but a God-inhabited society. Are we not reversing this ideal in an age when the Church still means in so many mouths the clergy, instead of meaning the Christian society, and when nine men are striving to get men to go to church for one who is striving to make men realise that they themselves are the Church?

There is no temple in the new Jerusalem. It is not a system of worship that Christianity came to bring to mankind; it is not a *religion*, as religion has usually been understood—a system of worship abstracted from the common life of men. It came to bind men together in just and true relations, to infuse into their societies the Divine spirit, to trans-figure the coarse vesture of humanity with that di-vinity which is love, till it shall become a temple in which He dwells. Its power is not that of a distant God who must be approached by special ceremonies, by special modes of life and thought, by shaping humanity into some peculiar attitude, but the power of a present God. The title of its Founder is Immanuel,

E 2

God with us, God in us, God making Himself a home
in all the relations by which love and justice draw man
to man, and class to class, and nation to nation ; a
God who is known and realised in the tenderness of
fatherly and motherly and filial affection, the rapture of
married love, the steadiness of friendship, the honesty of
trade relations, the loyalty of citizenship, the righteousness of political rule, the peace which is destined to bind
together all mankind. Where these exist there is God ;
where they are not He is absent. All worship which
does not aim at these is hypocrisy ; that worship alone
is Christian worship which tends to their establishment.

It is not a quibble or a verbal criticism to observe
that the vision of the Apocalypse represents the
nations which are saved as walking in the light of
the Holy City, as drinking of its waters, and being
healed by the leaves of the Tree of Life. It is not in
individuals that the fulness of the Gospel power is
realised, but in great societies of men. The body of
Christ is not the individual, but the company of
believers. The God whom we worship is not the bare
individual unity which some would assert, but the God
whose name is Love, the Father of Jesus Christ, the
Spirit who breathes through all things. And the image
of God upon earth is not the individual soul, which
cannot be made perfect by itself, but the society of
men who dwell in faith and love. This is the body
of Christ, the fulness of Him who filleth all in all.

And this society is no narrow one embracing but a
part of human life, satisfying one only, however deep,

of the functions of humanity, but that which embraces the whole range of human relations. It does not embrace only the gatherings of men for worship or for instruction or for beneficence, but comprehends that supreme corporate union which is termed the nation, which, by a Divine sanction, regulates all the relations of men, and from which there is no appeal. The nations, in which alone humanity can grow to completeness, must themselves become churches, provinces of the kingdom of God.

In the last sermon which it was my privilege to address to this audience I dwelt on faith as the great reuniter ; I pointed out how strange a spectacle was presented by the enmities arising among men in the name of Christianity, and showed that the reuniting power was faith, which in its simplicity, its versatility, its elevation, transcends or passes beyond those more limited views of religion which cause dissension, and holds fast as supreme the image of God presented to us in the character of Jesus Christ. But if this be granted, it may still be asked whether the outworking of faith must not make it pass into the phase in which it again becomes the subject of contention. Must it not work itself out into propositions, into concrete facts, into institutions, into that which St. Paul calls the dogmas and ordinances of men ? And must not these again, as the Jewish law in his day, become the ground of dissension and of enmity, and so must not the old evil return upon us ?

The answer to this difficulty which I gave in my

former sermon was that faith, the holding fast of the image of God presented in the character of Christ, is supreme, and that while we maintain it to be so, the special modes in which it is expressed, or the institutions in which men seek to realise it, are *comparatively* unimportant.   When we see the largeness and variety of faith, we are not induced to quarrel with one another by those things which are secondary to it ; we differ, but only as the various gifts of the Spirit may differ in those who confess that it is one Lord who worketh all in all.   But I wish to-day to point out that the enmity and contention arises from the fact that the working out of faith so often takes a wrong direction.   Faith is not best promoted when men try to realise it in a system of religious worship and teaching which is kept separate from the general aims of human life, instead of acknowledging as its chief sphere those plain human relations which form the life of mankind.   Religion, as a separate thing, alien from human relations, becomes, through this very enmity which it produces, abhorrent to men, and the conscience of mankind is being led to find rest in the working out of those principles which bind men together in society.   Christianity is destined, by the very law of its being, so to infuse itself into the societies and kingdoms of men that they may become the kingdoms of God and of Christ ; and while this is its aim, everything indicates that it will be welcomed more and more by the nations which are bent on living out their life in peace and justice and liberty.   The secular life lived in the Spirit of our Lord is the great point of reconciliation for a world which is weary of theological and ecclesiastical strife.

I pointed out in my previous discourse how simple a thing faith is, how it may almost be said to be independent of dogma. Wherever there is an aspiration after goodness, wherever there is sympathy with it, *there* is faith in Christ. We need not change or deny any of the dogmas in which Christian thought has clothed itself, but we insist that they should be interpreted in connection with moral goodness; for we may feel sure that what is most precious in God's sight, what is recognised by God as the truest faith, is the vital sentiment, the principle of a sacred life, which Christ came to build up, and which must underlie all that is said or done in His name. This faith, which is capable of universality, allies itself most readily with the secular life of man. We cannot expect the mass of men to take an interest in the technical parts of religion, in the details of the modes of worship, or the peculiar ways of expression on which most controversies turn. These are the professional business of a class—the ministers of public worship, the professed theologians. But every man, nay, every human being, can learn to do his duty as in God's sight, and in the Spirit of our Lord Jesus Christ; and the more each one is earnestly engaged in this effort, the more he will feel the need of the divine help, and the more he will lean with manly trust on the support of Christ and of the Holy Spirit. The contact of Christian

faith with the secular life is good for both. The one is
prevented from sinking into weak refinement, the other
is raised from its grossness to become the temple of God.

Can any one read the Gospels without preconcep-
tions about the organisation of the Church, and fail
to see that that on which our Saviour was intent was
the raising and purifying of the common life of men?
Whether we read the more directly practical accounts
of the synoptics or enter into the deeper tone of St.
John, the same truth appears. The spirituality of
the Sermon on the Mount is not that of meditation
and worship, and instruction about another world,
but of reality and depth of motive in all we do: the
direct teaching of our Lord is that of the Fatherhood
of God, the assurance of forgiveness, the brotherhood of man, the relations of the family, our be-
haviour towards the weak and sinful. The teaching
of the parables concerns the test of true disciple-
ship, and the working out of great moral principles
in the life of men and of societies. The deeper
teaching of St. John proclaims that He who thus
taught and pledged His life to His teaching was
essentially divine. Nor need we make a theological
mystery of the expression used as to His death, and
the blessed consequences which have flowed from it.

The meaning of the sacrifice of the Cross is that
self-devoting love, the surrender of the will to truth
and to God, is the one thing acceptable to the Father,
the one thing by which God and man are brought into
harmony. There are in Christ's teaching no ordinances

for public worship; the intimations of another world
are few and distant. Even the sacraments are federal
acts, connected primarily with social life rather than
with prayer. To gather from the gospels a system which
is solely or chiefly a system of public worship, and of instruction concerning the life to come, would be a strange
infatuation. All is directed to insure a present life of
righteousness and of love, a life lived in the realisation
of a present God, whose kingdom is here within us.

And this fact becomes clearer to us when we
consider our Lord as the founder of a society.
The calling of the twelve was not for public worship and for instruction in the mysteries of futurity,
but for the foundation of a society which was to
embrace the whole life of its members. That their
first business was to teach and persuade men was a
matter of necessity, though with it, even in their first
trial mission, healing and beneficence were conjoined,
if they had not even the first place. And as soon as
the society was formed, on the Day of Pentecost,
its adherents threw into it their all. The community
of goods was a witness that they joined the Church
not for worship and for instruction in relation to a
future world, but for the whole course of the life now
present. All their relations to their fellow-men were to
be Church relations, the arrangements for the serving
of tables, with all the mechanism which this involved
(the germ of the life of a perfect society) was in the
hands of the Apostles. The distinction which has
been so constantly and so fatally maintained between

things sacred and things secular was unknown to the early Church. The life of the Church was, as St. Paul says, in God the Father and His Son Jesus Christ.

The Church, then, was to be a society which tends to embrace the whole life of mankind, to bind all their relations together by a Divine sanction. As such it blends naturally with the institutions of common life—those institutions which because they are natural and necessary are therefore Divine. It asserts and realises itself not so much as a separate society, but rather in the institutions into which it infuses itself. It joins itself with the family, and the family itself becomes, for the time, the Church. It may take at another time the form of a sect of the Jews, or of one of the Hetæriæ of the Roman Empire. But wherever it is true to its primary object it presses on to embrace the larger society, in which the relations of human life have the fullest play ; it becomes the soul of the already-existing fabric, and transforms it into a Church. The Divine system of human government, of which St. Paul says that its ministers are ministers of God, can never be outside of its range. The Church may for a time be a separate society, aloof from the national life or government ; but this is an abnormal state of things, and the effort of the Church which is true to its Master must be not to maintain its separation, but to merge itself in the society which God has made, and to find itself again in making that society truly and freely Christian.

What it aims at is not the recognition by the nation of a worshipping body, governed by the ministers of public worship, which calls itself the Church, but that the nation and all classes in it should act upon Christian principle, that laws should be made in Christ's spirit of justice, that the relations of the powers of the state should be maintained on a basis of Christian equity, that all public acts should be done in Christ's spirit and with mutual forbearance, that the spirit of Christian charity should be spread through all ranks and orders of the people. The Church will maintain public worship as one of the greatest supports of a Christian public life ; but it will always remember that the true service, the λογικὴ λατρεία of Christians, is a life of devotion to God and man far more than the common utterance of prayer.

That this is not generally felt, even in our own Christian commonwealth, although every page of our public liturgy bears witness to the sacredness of public life, must be attributed to the insufficient scope which men accord to the belief in God and in Redemption. When we believe that God is the common Father, and that all men and all things which he has made are dear to Him, when we think that he is near to every one of us, and that in Him we live and move and have our being, then we cannot count any man or any thing common or unclean. We believe that there is a Divine element in each man and each object, and our constant effort must be to draw out this Divine element. And when we realise the full scope of Redemption this truth becomes more clear and more dear to the believing heart. Christ is the Saviour of all men ; Christ came to redeem the world in all its wide expanse. There is nothing under the broad vault of heaven which is not included in the all-embracing purpose which is expressed by St. Paul in these words, " That He might gather together in one all things in Christ, both which are in heaven and which are in earth." All societies of men, all occupations of men, all knowledge, all art, all the intercourse of men in society or in trades, all the relations of nations one to the other, are not merely to be influenced from without by a body established for the purpose of public worship, but to become functions of that great body which only in the fulness of its entire life is to be the home and the temple of God.

Towards this end then we must strive. And it is an end which is not so distant or impossible as some may think it. There never was a time or a country in which it so needed to be kept in view, and in which the possibilities of its incoming were so great, as the present time and our own country. If the object were confessed by the leaders of opinion, and set distinctly before the nation, the very fact of its recognition would bring us half way to its accomplishment. It may, no doubt, be said and felt that it is far too good to be true; men will say that it is impossible to attribute to ordinary men such faith as will thus transform society. And this, no doubt, is true, if we mean by faith a well-considered adherence to every article main-

tained in Christian confessions. But if faith be a moral
conviction, a sympathy, an aspiration towards better
things, it is not untrue to assert that the general conviction is on the Christian side, and it is not untrue to speak
of a nation as Christian. The nucleus by which its
deeper life is led is thoroughly imbued with the Christian
spirit even now. The spirit of faith is alive and operative, though it does not find full expression in words.

It might almost fill us with despair, when we
recognise this as the true vocation of the Christian
Church, to find those who teach in our Christian
assemblies so often occupied with the inculcation
merely of an individual piety, which hardly takes
account of the social and political life even of individuals, and shrinks from public affairs as from some
unhallowed thing. Religion is often praised for producing "an unearthly experience," its effect is often
to break up men's common life, and to send them, like
Arthur's knights, in ecstatic pursuit of the Holy
Grail, instead of staying like valiant men to bring the
world under the dominion of right ; and the ministers
of public worship are often more anxious to bind themselves together as a class and assert their separate life,
than to serve the community well ; their effort is often
to make public worship a function withdrawn from
the life of mankind, rather than the means of refresh-
ing and elevating that life ; they are often more
anxious to keep matters like education in their own
hands, than to strive that, in whosoever's hands, it
should be conducted so as to diffuse knowledge and

righteousness among the people ; the Church constantly means the clergy (as indeed it must until it
identifies itself with the nation), and this miscon-
ception makes the Church appear as the enemy of
human progress and the source instead of the assuager
of strife. These things might fill us with despair,
but for the certainty that the true kingdom of Christ
must come, and for the evidence of its coming which
we see both in history and in present society.

It was a noble effort that was made in the
Middle Ages by men like Hildebrand to bring all
Christendom into harmony. It was a brave attempt and a true foreshadowing of that which the
Church is designed to do. But though the attempt
was a noble one, and was motived by the belief
that the clergy were capable of regenerating the
world if the world were placed under their dominion,
it was based on a false calculation. It still kept life
divided into two distinct spheres, which were only
harmonised by the one being absolutely subject to the
other. The clergy and the so-called spiritual power
was everything. The laity and the so-called temporal
power was nothing. Moreover, an order separated by
celibacy from the general life were altogether incompe-
tent to rule. The monastic ideal was quite inadequate
to the task of influencing and regenerating the general
life. And had it been possible to subject all the
powers of Christendom to the clergy, and had the
clergy been as pure as they were corrupt, the result of
separating off one power, one function, in the Church,

and making it supreme over all the rest, would merely have been to emasculate the other powers, to deprive them of their sense of responsibility, and to substitute the false notions of clerical law for the demand for just rule which was slowly beginning to dawn. The clergy, who rejoiced to see the head of the secular power humbled before the Pope at Canossa, had done nothing, when the education of the young sovereign had been entrusted to them, to fortify him with kingly virtues; they presented to him the spectacle of worldly men, who used the privileges which they claimed to ensure their own wealth and power. In the strife of the clergy and the kingly power, there was indeed but little to make impartial men take either side; but the secular and equal justice of which the kings of England and of Germany were the guardians should be quite as dear to Christian hearts as the public worship and monastic virtues maintained by a Hildebrand or a Becket. To call the one temporal and the other spiritual, the one Christian, the other worldly, is a mistake, and the parent of a whole family of mistakes. For that which is Christian is simply that which is just.

In the conflicts of the clergy against the secular power in the present day, we find those who have the conduct of the government waking up gradually to the fact that they have a religious responsibility; that they, and not only the clergy, are ministers of religion. The religion of justice in human relations is taking its place side by side with the religion of

dogma and prayer; and the task of our age is to
harmonise them. Take such a country as Italy, the
centre of the clerical system. The regeneration of
Italy has been accomplished by the devotion of
men like D'Azeglio and Cavour, Mazzini, Garibaldi,
and Cadorna, in the teeth of the vehement opposition of the clergy. Some of these men had the
deepest respect even for the Roman Catholic system,
the excesses of which they combated; some of them
were antagonistic to that system. The writings
of .some of them, like Mazzini, cannot be read
without seeing that the fear of God was paramount with them. They were supported in their
conflict with the representatives of the clergy by a
religion as strong as theirs, the religion of human
justice. Liberty of worship, constitutional government, equality before the law, the abolition of
shackles upon the press and public meetings, universal education, the sanction of civil marriages, all
these form a body of doctrine quite as clear to men's
minds, quite as Christian, and far more operative on
the consciences of the mass of men, than any which
they heard taught in the churches. These formed a
real religion to them, which has stood the test of every
conflict, and has presented an instructive contrast to
the religion of the clergy. Read side by side the
Syllabus and the Italian Constitution, or compare
the utterances of Pius IX. with those of Italian
statesmen, and you cannot doubt that the true religion lies on the side of the latter. There is a strange

story of Garibaldi being asked on one occasion when on a journey to give his blessing to an infant child of an Italian patriot. He took the child in his arms, and kissed it, and sprinkled water upon it, and said that he baptised it into the brotherhood of Italian unity. That may have struck some as a blasphemous act, as a parody of Christianity. May we not rather view it as the dawning of a larger and truer Christianity—a Christianity which knows that the brotherhood of men is as sacred as the Fatherhood of God, which esteems every act of public and private righteousness as an act of religion, and feels that the ministers of human justice and liberty are, as well as the ministers of prayer and preaching, the ministers of 'Jesus Christ our Lord?

It has been the happiness of our own country to avoid to some extent the conflicts on these points which have been so rife in Europe. Yet there is very great fear lest through a narrow, unbending attitude on the part of the clergy, a disastrous confusion and conflict may be brought on. There has been among us a tendency to keep under the control of the ministers of public worship matters which quite as rightly fall under the control of the ministers of civil justice. It was quite right that the clergy should urge their flocks to undertake such works, nay, should conduct them themselves if they were not taken up by others. But the danger comes when the clergy, who can carry on such things at best but imperfectly, show a jealousy of their being taken up by others, and

F

raise a cry that the Church is in danger, and form a
Church party to support it, in opposition to that
which is felt as a necessity by the conscience of a
Christian nation.   What we ought to do is to strive
that the nation should act in a really Christian sense.
As it is we are constantly setting the clergy (or, as
men usually but erroneously speak, the Church) in
opposition to the nation.   We are jealous of laws
being made by the nation itself in Parliament for the
regulation of Church affairs, though these are the
affairs of the whole nation; we cannot endure the
making of just laws concerning marriage by the
Legislature, because they may interfere with the
observance of certain ecclesiastical ideas about marriage.   We are cold in* our appreciation of the
educational efforts of the last ten years, because they
may detract from the clerical hold on education in
the towns.   And we are unwilling that our Christian brethren who do not worship with us should
lie side by side with our adherents in the grave.*
We are jealously apprehensive of popular movements
because they may interfere with the privileges of the
clergy as a great conservative class.   And all this we
do because we unduly magnify the ministry of public
worship, which we identify with the Church, and
unduly mistrust the Christian character of the community, which we thus in our thoughts treat,
and almost compel to become, unchristian.   The

* This was preached some eighteen months before the passing of
the Burials Act.

result is that step by step the ground is, and justly, won which we try in vain to defend. The administration of the legal relief of the poor has been taken out of clerical hands, and that of ·charitable relief will very possibly leave them also. The registrar's marriage office confronts the Church, and it is very possible that marriage before the registrar may become compulsory. Church schools are rivalled by Board schools, and many good judges believe that the Church schools must eventually succumb. And all this is done not by revolutionists, but with full Christian conviction by the great organs of the national will. And if the still greater change comes which has been made in Ireland, and which some believe to be imminent in England, it will be, let us take good heed to it, not from any repudiation of Christianity and of the Church by an apostate nation, nor because men believe in a separation of things secular from things sacred (a separation in the nature of things impossible, and the idea of which is a heathen idea which Christianity came to dispel), but because the Christian nation, acting with full conviction as a Church in defence of its Christian life, can no longer endure a clerical organisation which has become an unbrotherly influence and a perpetual incentive to unchristian disunion.

And while the religion which finds its expression only in worship and in dogmas, and in the hopes and fears of futurity, seems to divide men hopelessly from each other, so that the organisations formed for these

F 2

purposes follow their own way without regard to each other, the general interests of man's present life, which, if conducted unselfishly, are Christian and eternal interests, are drawing men powerfully into union. The national life in all its branches, and the blessedness of the brotherhood which it imparts, the pursuit of genuine knowledge, of art, of invention, the work of philanthropy, are points in which those can readily meet who are alienated by clerical discord. These things, no doubt, if conducted in a selfish and worldly spirit, may become unchristian (as indeed the functions of the clergy may also become); but if they are conducted in the spirit of Christian justice and love they are the genuine functions of the Christian Church, genuine products of the Christian life. In many of them there is little or no controversy; in all of them men can meet and discuss as brethren, maintaining a higher unity beyond all their differences; while in the realm administered by the clergy men are almost compelled to admit that their differences are irreconcilable, and that they must keep each other for ever apart.

The tendency of our argument may seem to some to be to increase the antagonism between the two spheres, and to raise up the so-called secular life at the expense of the so-called Church life. But this is not so. We wish to point out the sacredness of that which is called the secular life, so that the whole life of men, with all its functions, may be brought under the dominion of Christ, that there may be no breach between prayer and work, between religion and know-

ledge, between clergy and laity, between Church and
State; that the Fatherhood of the Creator may be
recognised as universal in the brotherhood of His
children, that the Redemption of Christ may be
acknowledged as the saving power in all branches
and functions of human energy. Moreover, I am
persuaded that, if this be once acknowledged to the
full, the result of it will be, not an undervaluing of
the work which is the special function of the clergy,
but a fuller recognition of its importance. Those
who work side by side with the same motives in
matters of philanthropy or politics, acknowledging
the supremacy of our Lord, will not be content
without worshipping together. Those who acknowledge that the sanction which makes their work a
noble service is the belief in God, will want to hear
more about God, and will return to theology and its
teachings with a new zest. Those who are constantly
dealing with the mysteries of human life, with a view
to gain fresh knowledge and to elevate mankind, will
not be content to be stopped by the barriers of sense
and time, but will long and aspire together to the
eternal world and to the life to come. It is not to
plead the cause of knowledge or secular politics
against piety that we preach, but to embrace in the
circle of piety the whole life of man.

I therefore, in conclusion, make an appeal: 1st
to the clergy; 2nd, to the laity.

1. I entreat the clergy not to make their minis-
trations exclusive, and this in two senses, both as

regards the Christian bodies outside their own organisation, and as regards the laity generally. I do
not enter into the differences between Christians, but
I am quite sure that they are greatly exaggerated.
I believe that Christian hearts, if they only knew
more of each other, would beat more in unison. If
the great needs of our people are considered, we can
rejoice in the good done by others than ourselves,
and we can learn to honour men according to the
real amount of Christian good which they accomplish.
And all that this implies is that we should cease from
the attitude of supercilious ignorance which we are
apt to assume towards them, and should recognise
and take an interest in their good works. Look not
every man on his own things, but every man also on
the things of others. And, as to the laity, let us
learn to think of them as having each a ministry to
fulfil, according to the words of one of our prayers,
"That every member of the whole body of the
Church in his vocation and ministry may truly and
godly serve the Lord." Let us give up utterly the
separation of things sacred and things secular. Let
our great aim be to stimulate knowledge and art and
political good, and all the culture which ennobles
human life, to urge upon all men to conduct their
common work as a function of the Church of God,
to bring the great sanctions of the invisible world to
bear upon the elevation of mankind.

2. I urge this also on the laity with all earnestness. It would be impossible at the close of a

sermon to show in detail the application of our principles to the various branches of secular life. But a few words may be said as to the actual business of this University. It is said that the changes of late years have made the teaching-staff less clerical and the whole atmosphere less theological. It does not follow, I trust, that Oxford is less a place of religious education. Men are no longer kept under the restraint of a clerical system which permitted only such a course of study as seemed consonant with its own interests. But if, as testimony seems to show, those who study here do so more diligently, if truth comes with freedom, if mutual toleration ensues on a frank recognition of differences, the University is not less but more a place of Christian learning. It is not so much the subject of study as the spirit in which it is pursued that makes it Christian or un-Christian. This is the crucial question. About this, I pray you, let there be no hesitation. Let those who follow research do so with truth for their aim, and with such a regard for their fellows as will make them give out freely the results of their research; then, but not otherwise, their study will be Christian study. Let those who teach make it their object to perfect themselves in an art for which no previous training is provided, and which is often very imperfectly acquired by practice, and let them show by many kindly offices their interest in the welfare of those they teach—so alone will they be Christian teachers. Let those who are learning be really in earnest to acquire knowledge, and to fit themselves for their future career, and be careful in their conduct and example. These things will render the teachers and students of this University, though there may be among them fewer ministers of worship than of old, real ministers of Christ to pupils or to comrades on whose welfare they have an influence. And if at the present it is found that some ordinances of religion, like the daily prayer in chapel, are less largely frequented than when they were compulsory, let me urge that there is a compensatory service which all can render in the maintenance of a high sense of duty, in fostering the inner life in a religious spirit, in mutual care and interest. And let the hope be maintained that, if the common worship of God endures some suspension for a time, it may be for a time only. It cannot be but that, in the freedom of study and discussion, many divergent ideas should arise about those things which, precious as they are, must ever seem subject to much uncertainty, and which are the object of faith and hope rather than of exact knowledge. But do not carry these divergencies on one side or the other so far as to hinder sympathy and co-operation in your proper work. Let the sympathy you have in one of the noblest of human employments draw you together into common hopes, common aspirations ; and we may yet see here a better society than that which the religion of worship alone would give, the society of a life lived out under the spiritual dominion of Christ.

III.

The Supremacy of Christ over the Secular Life.

III.

The Supremacy of Christ over the Secular Life.

(Preached before the University of Oxford, April 27, 1879.)

"Thou sayest that I am a King."—JOHN xviii. 36.

"All power is given unto me in heaven and in earth."—
MATTHEW xxviii. 18.

IT has been sometimes said of late years that Christianity has resigned the leadership of the world, and that the friends of humanity must now step in to act as a natural Providence and conduct the affairs of the race. There is some truth in the complaint, whatever we may think of the proposed remedy. For there has been at all times a tendency among Christians to abandon the claim of universal sovereignty which was at first made in the name of their Lord. The claim may be made in words, but left in a purely ideal state; and when no attempt is made to give it a practical application, it is in effect abandoned. A Christianity which embraces but a part of human life, while it adjourns its fuller claim to the world beyond the grave, is certainly not the religion of One who says, "All power is given unto me in heaven and in earth."

Jesus Christ is all in all. His followers cannot

be content to claim for Him anything less than sovereignty. We may dispute about the precise mode in which that sovereignty is to be expressed, and may not be content with the theological terms in which past ages have defined it. We may admit that those who have sought to enforce this sovereignty as a practical thing at various times have failed. But the failure has been due to the mistakes of later times, not to the falsehood of the original claim. Such failures cannot destroy the truth of the claim, or its practical character. Christ is still the Son of God, and the true King of mankind, and of the universe. For us, as for St. Paul, "though there be gods many, and lords many, there is but one Lord Jesus Christ, by whom are all things, and we by Him."

The end towards which we look is not that all men should be bound to certain rules of life, nor that they should all be alike in the public worship of God, nor that the anticipation of the world to come should overpower the duties and interests of the present; but that all human life should be lived out under the dominion of Christ. This, which has sometimes been confessed in words, has rarely been steadily contemplated in fact. The dominion of Christ has been looked upon as if it were like the rule of an earthly king, who guides the outer life, but cannot reach the inner; or, again, by a revulsion to the opposite extreme, as if it were merely a spirit or sentiment which hardly cares for the body or the general life. And as to the means by which it is to be enforced,

men have varied from the advocacy of stern com-
pulsion to that of simple persuasion. But, in truth,
the design of Christianity is this, that human life
should be lived out with perfect freedom, but under
the empire of the master motive of love, in the fear of
God, in the belief of His fatherly redeeming mercy.
And the means by which this is to be attained
embrace all the methods by which human life is
conducted. The spirit of the Gospel sets free all the
faculties, it inspires them with the energy of love;
and it accepts all the means which the free life of
mankind invents for reaching that development. So
far as man is an individual, so far Christianity is an
individual influence. So far as man is a social being,
Christianity is social. If man requires laws, the
Christian spirit can enter with those laws. If there
are parts of human life which must always lie beyond
the reach of law, Christianity vindicates that exemp-
tion from law, and furnishes men with a stimulus and
safeguard from a higher source than that of law. If
it be true that man is utilitarian, what is this but that
the Father of Jesus Christ wishes all his children to
aim at each other's happiness? If idealism has a
place, as it must have, even in the most utilitarian
system, does not a follower of Christ hear the voice
of his Lord saying to him constantly, "I came to
bear witness to truth; he that is of truth heareth my
voice;" or, again, "Be perfect as your Father in
heaven is perfect;" or, again, " My kingdom is not of
this world."

It has been maintained at times that Christianity is concerned with conduct, and conduct only, and its vindication has been rested by a writer of striking originality on the ground that conduct is three-fourths or perhaps seven-eighths of human life. But do we pass out from the Divine influence of our Lord, when we come to the other fourth or eighth part, when we go beyond the limits of the serious and moral view of life ?   In the realms of art or of music, which are so restful to the human spirit, has Christ nothing to say to us ?   In purely literary pursuits, or those of abstract science, does the human spirit range apart from His ?   In recreation and in mirth are we no longer His disciples ?   Is the only question to be asked as to any course of action, how does this bear on the regulation of conduct ?   Or if we get beyond that question, are we wandering without a guide ?   If that were so, I cannot see how religion should be the supreme power of life, or Christ its King.   There would be a double spirit, or indeed many spirits, at work within us.   We should have to make a distinction between Christ and the Father, as Goethe did when he made Werther say, " Perhaps I am not one of those whom the Father has given to Christ, but one of those whom the Father has kept for Himself;" or we should have to divide ourselves between God and no God, to consecrate parts of our time and our faculties as Theistic, and acknowledge the rest as Atheistic.   Can human life be thus bisected ?

We want a larger definition of faith, and a larger

conception of the spirit of Christ. If faith be the
acceptance of statements about God and Christ and
the future life, it is true that it cannot be universal.
But if it be, as I have maintained on former occasions,
a trust in the Father of whom Christ is the image, a
sympathy with goodness, an aspiration towards the
blessed life, such a faith as this can enter into every
part of the soul, like the air which pervades the whole
surface of the globe, and gives life to all that breathes
and grows upon it.

I desire to show that Christ's spirit is the true
guiding power in all spheres of human activity ; that
it is not only an inspiring motive, but also suggests
the right end to aim at. It must be so if we believe
in a redemption for humanity ; for that redemption
points to and ensures a blessed state, a holy city, a
divine society, in which God shall dwell with men.
In that state can we suppose that anything which is
good can be left out ? Has the New Jerusalem
neither statues, nor pictures, nor stately architecture,
nor dramas, nor games ? Is it to be, as M. Renan
says of the New Jerusalem of the Revelation, a gaudy
and tasteless toy ? Or, as might appear from some
religious ideals, are its boys and girls to laugh no
more, or its citizens to exercise their minds in no
problems but those of morals and sociology ? If such
suppositions are impossible, then all who look for a
complete redemption must seek to realise the Divine
influence in all parts of life, whether grave or gay,
whether so-called secular or sacred. They must

begin here, and now, to build up the fabric of a blessed life, which comprehends the whole organisation of a perfect society, ruled by Christ's justice, and inspired by His love.

It will be best, for the purposes of this sermon, to show how this is to be worked out in detail in those spheres of life which are supposed to have least connection with religion. I will take several of these and point out, not mere'y how the Spirit of Christ may connect itself with them, but how it suggests the object to be aimed at, and presides over the method of reaching it.

1. Here in Oxford let me begin with education. And this is especially appropriate, because the divorce of religion and education is loudly proclaimed in certain quarters, after a long and not inharmonious marriage. "The school for the state, and the Church for God," is the specious but misleading formula in which this divorce has been expressed. What is really meant by this is that the ministers of public worship are no longer to control education. But is there anything in the Christian religion which makes it necessary that the ministers of public worship should control either teaching or research? Is it not much truer to say that public worship is one function or ministry, and the training of youth is another? Is it not a wider and juster view of the Church, which embraces the several ministries as several, than that which would subject all its divers functions to a single order? Let education, if so it be found con-

venient, be conducted without clerical supervision; absolutely so if necessary. In what way does that expel Christ and His Spirit from it? May there not be real conscientious religion in a lay teacher? Even if the teaching of Scripture and the use of prayers were made impossible by our unfortunate differences, that would not make the education unchristian. The care of teachers for pupils, the reverence of pupils for teachers, the common sense of duty, and the sympathy which is engendered by a common work—this is the religion of education. I know not what Christianity demands more than this. Even where, as in America, the almost total exclusion of direct religious teaching from the schools has been attempted, it is found that the spirit of a Christian teacher communicates itself irresistibly to the pupils, and that, even as to religious observances which go on outside the schools, the pupils very commonly follow their teacher. But in our country there is no reason why direct Christian teaching should be excluded. If the spirit of Christian liberality prevails to abate our differences, all that is essential in the way of Christian knowledge can be communicated to the mass of the pupils. Nor is there any reason why the ministers of public worship should not bear in this a conspicuous and fruitful part. But this the spirit of Christ demands, that truth, unfettered by prejudices, whether of the clergy or of any other class, preside over the whole process.

Does the freedom of truth and of love, then, mean that there is to be no system, no guidance? Is

G

education and research to go on by desultory, spas-
modic, arbitrary impulses? By no means. Christianity is a cosmic as well as a spiritual faith. It has
to do with the universe as well as the human spirit.
The power of its Lord is over all in heaven and earth.
The sense of harmony which love produces extends
itself over the whole creation. The Christian Scriptures throughout place man as the spiritual centre of
a world in which all things find their place in subor-
dination to him. Christ is the centre of mankind,
and mankind is the centre of the world. If that be
so, we have a central point round which all knowledge
groups itself. The physical and the moral sciences
have each their part in the building up of the great
human temple in which God dwells ; and the highest
education is that which gives men a complete conception of the world thus viewed, as centred in
humanity and in Christ, its head. Or if this be taken
on the practical side, the true education is that which
fits a man to bear his part aright among his fellow-
men, in the society of which the central principle is
love, and which acknowledges Christ as the supreme
expression of that love. Thus the spirit of Christ
asserts itself as the master power in the sphere of
education.

2. Let us pass to a sphere which is commonly
dealt with as being far removed from directly
Christian influences, and which is hardly touched by
ordinary Christian teaching. I mean the sphere of
trade. It is said by those who speculate upon the

future, that commerce, which already is so absorbing
a pursuit, is destined to grow to far larger dimensions.
And this can hardly fail to be the case in England,
whether England or America bear the palm of the
trade of the future. It is commonly and thought-
lessly assumed that men sell to make their fortunes,
and buy to feed and clothe themselves. Is that a
true and sufficient account of dealings which occupy
a large part of every life? Even so, the question is
whether this is done honestly. And it is pretty
certain that if there be no motive at work but the
pursuit of our own convenience on one side, and of gain
on the other, convenience and gain will be degraded into
greed and dishonesty. You want a constant motive
to raise trade from mere chaffering into dignity, and
this motive Christianity supplies. It is evident that
trade cannot exist without fair dealing. But where
there is fair dealing there is room for love; and if so
there ought to be love. Here then is an entrance for
the Christian spirit into the whole system of commer-
cial exchanges; and where the Christian spirit enters
it at once asserts its supremacy. The higher motive
drives out the lower; what you are doing for love you
can do no longer merely for gain.

The ideal to which this motive points is this: that
the trader should have for his first object to supply
the wants of those about him, and should follow this
out, not merely so far as it will bring him gain, but
to the full extent of his ability. Does this sound
Utopian? Is it certain that a man who should do

this would be ruined? On the contrary, everything tends to show that one who should set to work in this way would conciliate the confidence and support of all men ; for if it were once known that this was his object, who would not rather deal with him than with any other? Nor is this mere speculation. The new system of co-operative trading, which is known to be in the interest of those who buy, not merely in that of those who sell, even when carried out to the very limited extent of plain honesty guaranteed by imme-diate payment, is threatening all trade which is carried on on other systems, and where it goes further, and gives an interest to the buyer in all that he purchases, it must of necessity carry all before it. The greatest retail establishment which the world has ever seen—the great store in New York, the proprietor of which died some two years ago—was founded on this principle, to give to the public none but the best articles, and to give them at the lowest rate which would ensure the carrying on of the business. He who wrought upon this principle, so far from being ruined, made the largest fortune ever realised by a retail trader. So literally true is the saying of Christ, "With what measure ye mete withal, it shall be measured to you again."

And if we follow out this thought, it leads us beyond what is possible now to that which may become possible if the Christian spirit can fully assert itself. The brotherly spirit of the Gospel must favour the extension of co-operation, whether in the production or the distribution of goods. And beyond this, perhaps, there will dimly dawn upon our view a state of things in which the Christian community itself should minister to all the wants of all its members, in which love and energy, with a moderate assured remuneration, might supply the motive power which is now supplied by eager competition and the prospect of excessive gain. It is a dream, no doubt, but only such a dream as it might have been to past generations, that the community might one day carry its own letters, or transmit its own messages, or lay up the savings or conduct the insurances of its poorer members, or that there might be a scheme, regarded by many with favour, by which all the great iron roads might be possessed by the community for the advantage of the citizens. To act upon such a dream or anything like it as if the Christian spirit were strong enough now to realise it would be madness. To attempt to enforce it, as Socialists have attempted to enforce their schemes, would be not folly only, but tyranny. But to work towards it by infusing into all trade the spirit of beneficence and mutual confidence, of trust-fulness and of unselfish generosity, is to prepare the way of Christ in one vast and growing province of His dominion.

3. I come now to another field, that of literature. With this too it is often thought that Christ has no connection. There may be literature which is about Christ, it is thought, but the literature itself, the form,

the art of it, has nothing to do with Christ. And the genuine literary man lives in the form itself: his pabulum is not the substance but the form in which it is clothed.

But is it possible to make this absolute severance between matter and form? May it not rather be said that, apart from the matter, the form cannot maintain its worth? It was a great truth which was touched by Schleiermacher when he spoke of the language-forming power of Christianity. The Gospels (to take the first and most central instance), have a great literary charm in their simplicity, in their freshness and *naiveté*. But who can say that their form is independent of their subject matter? Much more truly we may say that it is the fact that the writers were dealing with a subject so divine and yet so simple that gives the divine simplicity to their form. The spirit of Christ is in the form as well as the matter, in the grace, in the chasteness, in the reticence, in the short uninvolved sentences like those of a child, in the naturalness and directness of the style. This is confessed by writers like M. Renan—no mean judge, assuredly, of literary style, who turns with delight to the synoptic gospels as breathing the fresh air of the Galilean hills, and who similarly compares the impression which we receive in reading the Acts of the Apostles to that which we gain in reading the Odyssey.

It is not so always, no doubt; there may be a grace which has lost all hold of reality. It is like the

resemblance we sometimes trace in the outward form
and manners of the degenerate child to those of his
nobler parents, or like gracious words and outward
courtesy covering a bad heart. This does not dis-
prove the truth that qualities are transmitted by race,
or that it is a loving heart that is the true parent of
courtesy. And, similarly, it is the love which is the
nature of God and of Christ which in one or other
of its forms is the true inspirer of literature. No
genuine or original style has ever been formed where
there was no deep human sympathy, but only a
playing with words.

Moreover, literature, what is it ? It is a form of
expression. Not only is expression dependent on the
thing to be expressed, but the wish to express is the
correlative of the wish to impress. We want to
express our thoughts in writing as in speech, in order
that they may reach home to other minds, that they
may evoke sympathy, and inspire noble thoughts, and
incite to generous action. This has been the kindling
spark of all the highest literary genius.

We may raise the matter to a higher point. If all
human nature is redeemed by Christ, then every
human excellence is part of the process. The very
fact that literature is part of this excellence in itself
makes it Christian. Aim at excellence, and you are
aiming at what Christ designed. If this is true any-
where, it must be doubly true where we are dealing
with human speech, the organ of the human spirit,
through which the divine breath breathes out upon

mankind. . Get rid of the idea that secular literature is to be enslaved to ecclesiasticism, and you have no difficulty in accepting for it the sovereignty of Christ. The word of man cannot but be under the control and subject to the inspiring, redeeming influence of Him who, because his human life expressed the divine, is called the Word of God.

4. We may extend this thought to the whole province of art. Who can maintain that art is not a necessary part of human excellence? Would any one be so mad as to wish to banish it, as Plato banished the poets from his republic? If art is imitative, it is because man is an imitative being, and redemption must redeem this quality of imitativeness, not destroy it. It may be the shadow of a shadow of the true idea. But, nevertheless, the true idea stands out much more clearly to the apprehension of men through the medium of this shadow than it would if we saw the reality in its nakedness. Truth barely stated is apt to become truism. The bare light dazzles and kills; its refraction and disintegration show it in its true and enlightening glory. Even the most direct teaching needs some medium of metaphor. Our Lord Himself used parables. And so it is with all the arts, with architecture, and sculpture, and painting, with music or the drama. They partake of the nature of sacraments; the inward spiritual grace which they express is hidden and yet revealed by them. The circuit of the electric chain is long, but the spark is none the less vivid, none the less quickening.

Art needs reality at every turn. Divorce it from real life and it becomes but the bloom of decay. It is quite possible, no doubt, that there may be ages that are very real, and yet are without art ; for art is an excellence, a virtue, which seems to need special conditions, and these conditions are not always at hand. But if in some of the noblest art periods you have the germs of decay, which are developed in the succeeding age, what does that prove but that the reality which inspired the one was wanting to the other, and that as with an effete civilisation which needs re-invigorating through a process of revolution, a new departure must be taken by a new recourse to reality ?

Art gives rest to the soul. Does that make it less Christian ? Because we seem to be drawn away, among nymphs or landscapes, or the spectacle of men of other climes and ages, from the crushing sense of our responsibility, are we therefore outside the sphere of His influence who said " Come unto me and I will give you rest ?" could it be said that recreation was no part of even the most saintly life ? And if saintliness needs refreshment, humanity in all its parts needs art. It is quite impossible that this element of life can be out of the range of the Redeemer of mankind. And if the times in which art has been most highly developed have not been those in which Christianity has seemed most flourishing, the cause of this is to be found in the swaying to and fro which marks the progress of humanity. Take for instance the period of the Renaissance. What is it but a revolt against the exclusiveness of ecclesiasticism? We cannot look with much satisfaction on an age of moral unsettlement such as the Renaissance undoubtedly was. But Christian thought ranges over long periods, and awaits a full development in which the various elements of the complete excellence may be combined; and it is therefore prepared to see without complaint periods like the Renaissance or the eighteenth century which bring an infusion of a wholesome naturalism into the life which has been surcharged with elements like scholasticism, or the excess of ecclesiastical ritual and dogma.

And Christianity, even in its stricter and more limited aspect, constantly shows itself as the redeemer of art. By suggesting high aims, by presenting worthy characters and moving incidents, it draws out the nobler side of art, and prevents it from being degraded by sensualism and frivolity. Art, like every other sphere of human life, must recognise the great moral factors which in all departments are paramount.

And it would do so much more readily were it not for a certain antagonism which has been fostered by the narrower clerical influences, sometimes on the Catholic, sometimes on the Puritan side. How could sculpture thrive in a church like the Eastern, which counts it idolatrous? or how could any art but the austerest form of poetry flourish under the Puritan influence? Or how could the drama own the authority

of Christ under a system which denied Christian burial
to Molière ?　In these later days it is found that the
feeling for the drama has increased among Christian
people ; and it may well be hoped that to all the arts
a similar liberal policy may extend ; that so, while
remaining free, as they must ever be, they may in
their freedom own the beneficent influence of the
redeeming spirit of our Lord.

5. Is, then, the domain of the natural sciences
outside the pale and influence of Christianity? Is
this great realm, which to some minds seems to embrace the whole circle of human interests, or at least
to dwarf all others, outside the dominion of Christ ?
Is its growth destined to obliterate those spheres in
which Christian morality is seen to be rightfully
supreme ? I maintain, on the contrary, that those
spheres which we most readily associate with Christianity are paramount, while the natural sciences are
subservient to them ; and, also, that the sustaining
interest of the natural sciences is derived from those
spheres of human life which we more readily recognise
as subject to our Lord.

The various realms of knowledge and of interest
cannot for ever stand apart. There must be a co-
ordination of the sciences ; and if to some few minds
the natural sciences are everything, this we must
regard as a revolt from their former depression, and
as constituting only a temporary phase of thought.
The humanities, as they are rightly called, will in due,
time assert their supremacy. Every serious co-ordi-

nation of the sciences must be, with whatever minor adjustments, a reflexion of that which is assumed in the Scriptures; it must place man himself as the centre, and the rest as dependent upon him. It will always be much more important for us to know how we may live justly and love one another, than how material bodies are mutually attracted, or how the various parts of the universe came to be what they now are. We must, indeed, maintain that to neglect the natural sciences is to stunt human life, and we may thankfully recognise that the discoveries made in those sciences have greatly conduced to moral and religious good by giving us a truer understanding of the world in which we live. The true moralist will neglect no light which can be thrown upon human nature from the physical side. But the physicist must come to feel that his main interest centres in man. Before embarking in any enquiry, the mind almost irresistibly asks the question, to what good does this tend ? Will it conduce to human well-being? Mere curiosity and mere abstract aimless impulses will not sustain a man in the tedious pursuit of knowledge. He looks for his reward in the enlightenment, the advantage, the beauty which he may shed by his discoveries upon the path of his fellow-men. Would astronomy be worth pursuing were it not that it reveals to us some of the primary conditions of our existence in this planet ? Would chemistry be the absorbing pursuit which it is to its votaries without the assurance that organic chemistry is a step towards life and morals? What makes us await each new discovery in physiology but that it implicates human nature? Are not all these sciences so entrancing because they, from various sides, approach the problem of problems, the nature and origin of life? And does not the delight which the mind receives from the growing probability of the doctrine of evolution, lie in the promise which it seems to give of binding all, human and non-human, into one great Cosmos? If that be so, then human life is that to which all has been working upwards from the beginning; the Word and the Spirit, to use religious language, presided over the construction of the world; or, to use the language of one of the greatest of our men of science, the promise and potency of human life lay in the primeval elements waiting for its development. Christ is the head of humanity; and, if all knowledge centres in humanity, it centres in Christ. What is this but to say that Christ is its king?

6. Lastly, it might seem easy to vindicate for our Lord a sovereignty over all the relations of human beings, who are bound together by justice and by love. But there is a strange tendency to limit his empire even here; and, stranger still, this limitation often comes from his professed followers and ministers. God and Cæsar are set in antagonism. It is believed by many that the sphere of politics can be dissevered from that of religion, and this has been made the ground of theories which, whether they come from

the clerical or the secular side, are equally godless.
It cannot be that the public life, the natural home of
justice, should be separate from the God whose very
nature is righteousness.   If we can but bring ourselves to acknowledge that justice itself is pleasing to
God, and that what is most important is not the
naming of Christ's name, but the doing of the things
which embody his mind, we shall not fail to perceive
that the political life of mankind is even now under
Christ's supreme direction.

Take the three most remarkable political phe-
nomena of our own generation, and this will be made
clear.

The first of these is the triumph of constitutional
government throughout Europe.   We who are but
middle-aged men can remember the time when every
European nation but our own was under personal rule.
Italy, Hungary, France, Spain, Austria, Prussia, had all
the same tale to tell.   Now they all tell another tale ;
they are all self-governed.   But what is constitutional
government ?   It is only the expression in public
affairs of the Christian sentiments of justice and love.
Is it not equitable that nations as soon as they have
outgrown the state of childhood should rule themselves ?   Can any one, starting from the Christian
principle of equity, fail to recognise that it is not the
will of a single man which ought to impose itself on
the whole society, but that the society itself should
rule ?   Is it not, again, exactly in accordance with
Christian principle that the ruler should not be one

who forces his own authority upon the rest, but one who suggests, advises, persuades, and finally leads with the consent of the rest? Is not this the very spirit of the words, "neither as lords over God's heritage, but as ensamples to the flock?" And what is the impulse which has procured the gradual extension of the suffrage but the Christian wish to take into consultation all who are affected by the policy of the state, so that not even the interests of one of the little ones of the flock shall be neglected? It is often taken for granted that the organisation for public worship where this is not done is under Christ's direction, but that secular politics in which it is done are not. The contrary is the case. Christ is, and he reigns, where justice and love bear rule.

The second notable progress accomplished during this generation is the recognition of the principle that no nation should domineer over another. Greece and Italy, Hungary and Germany, are all cases in which this has been acknowledged; and now the other nations comprised in European Turkey are being added to the list one by one. And even England, in the plenitude of its imperialism, is fain to acknowledge that in India its power must be vindicated, not as a conquest but a tutelage. Here again we have Christian justice asserting itself.

A third progress, which is a progress rather in hope than in fulfilment, is some bond of agreement and co-operation among the great Christian nations of the west, which may tend to diminish wars, and to raise the weaker members of the commonwealth of nations. That there have been great wars in our time is true; but the difference between these wars and those of the last century is this, that in the last century men fought for territory and power, and, whether they gained these or lost them, the wars were simply evil; whereas in our day, every war has been for some great cause, and has resulted in good. The Crimean war resulted in the destruction of a tyrannical influence which weighed on all Europe, the Italian war in the unity of Italy, the American war in the abolition of slavery, the war of 1866 in the expulsion of Austria from Italy and Germany, the war of 1870 in the termination of the Napoleonic régime in France and in Europe and the unification of Germany, the war of 1877 in the liberation of the nationalities oppressed by the Turks. But it is beginning to be felt that war is a terrible evil of which Christendom should be ashamed. We cannot contentedly regard it, as was done in a famous sermon from this pulpit, or as in the inscription on a gun of Louis XIV., as *ultima ratio regum*, the final argument of kings. We want some method which will dispense with bloodshed as the ultimate appeal of Christian rulers. We have ourselves, in the Alabama Arbitration, made one successful essay in the better path, by which war has been avoided and jealousy almost eradicated between two Christian nations. And in the Congress of Berlin we have again substituted the arbitrament of argument for that of the sword.

What do these things mean, but that Christian equity and kindness are gradually coming to be acknowledged, or in other words that Christ is asserting His empire over the whole domain of political life?

I have three remarks to make in conclusion.

1. What I have endeavoured to assert, the claim of Christ to rule, nay, the actual progress of his dominion, will seem to many overstrained. The reason why this seems to be so is that you have identified Christ with clericalism or ecclesiasticism. It is not, I repeat, the rule of the clergy, nor the supremacy of public worship, nor of the thought of another life, nor of theology, nor of the opinions which have been commonly taken as Christian, that we have advocated, but the supremacy of Christ, of His spirit, of His righteousness and His love.

A book was published some fourteen years ago which professed to be the history of rationalism in Europe. It showed how one by one various spheres such as those on which I have dwelt to-day had liberated themselves from certain unjust or unreasonable ideas, which had for a long time dominated in the name of Christianity. The equivocal title of the work made it seem as though the process which was described was the taking away of each sphere in succession from under the dominion of Christ, in the interest of the dominion of human reason. But there is no conflict between Christ and human reason. What has been called the sweet reasonableness of Christ is as applicable to all

H

these spheres as it was to that of Judaic morals. The process which was described was really the winning back of each sphere in succession from childishness, or ignorance, or injustice, or prejudice, or from a mere belated conservatism which had clothed itself with the Christian name, to Christ himself, who is human reason in its noblest form. If Christianity is to be identified with what in a vague manner is called clericalism, it must perish; or, since it is imperishable, it must clothe itself in a new form more like itself. But if clericalism means all that was combated in the history of rationalism, it is really un-Christian in the highest degree. It is the voice of Christ, not that of a secular politician, which is saying to Europe " Clericalism—that is the enemy." Over the prostrate body of such clericalism as that Christ is advancing to the empire of the world.

2. The dominion which we claim for our Lord is not a restraint, but a stimulus. We who are the children of Christian Constitutionalism have learnt, a little earlier than the other nations, that government is not restraint but the free expression of the life of the society. We are expecting in our rulers, and finding in some few of them, a leadership in works of utility which free our commerce, and facilitate the expansion of industry, and promote temperance and thrift and knowledge. That which we expect in our rulers we find in Christ. " I am a King," He said, " because I bear witness to truth, and all truthful souls follow me." When we say that Christ is King

in each of the spheres on which we have touched, we do not mean that these spheres are to be subjected to some external power, but that each of them, by the free development of its proper principle of life, is to become more and more a field for the exercise of truth and love. St. Paul said, "Whatever gift we have, let us *wait upon it*," that is, let us exercise it it according to its proper development—"whether ministering, let us wait on our ministering : or he that teacheth, on teaching ; he that ruleth, let him do it with diligence," and so with the other functions of the Christian life. So we may say, whatever sphere of life you move in, fill that sphere according to its own need and strive after its proper virtue and excellence, and you will make it Christ's.

And thus we do not want merely to negotiate a strained concordat between Christianity and other spheres of life, but to bring to bear upon every sphere an elevating and redeeming influence. Our Christianity must not be content to be found barely compatible with human progress. It must take the lead. It must bear the flag at the head of the advancing column. It must have an appropriate message for every class of men. It must appreciate art as art, knowledge as knowledge, literature as literature, politics as politics. It must urge them to excellence. It must set the highest standard before them. It must welcome every new fact that is laid bare, every new invention, every production of art, every extension of commerce, every great

H 2

literary work, every development of political freedom. It must do more; it must call for these incessantly, and stimulate men in the search for them. It must shew its Christ-like love for men by leading them on to triumph.

3. This reign of Christ of which we have spoken, the reign about which His last injunctions were given in the forty days between Easter and Pentecost, must be enforced in Christian teaching. We have been too long at the threshold, thinking how salvation may be won and sin forgiven, too little in the Palace itself where Christ reigns. The difficulty which meets us everywhere when we seek to bring the world under Christ's authority is to infuse the higher motive where so much is inert, and there is such a tendency to sluggishness and even to revert to some former and lower type. But it is to this that Christian teaching must apply itself. It must treat mankind as having become the subjects of Christ's redemption, it must assert His reign in detail over each sphere in which He is King. A former age produced the Religio Medici. We must have in this age the religion of art, the religion of science, the religion of the drama, the religion of trade. The problem for the ministers of Christianity lies here, to make it effective in all the walks of life in which a man moves. If dogmas trouble you, let dogmas alone for the time. But your life must be lived here and to-day; and if it is to be in the right it must be inspired by Christ's spirit. Learn to say to your-

self, " All that I do, I do for God in gratitude for His fatherly love." When your eyes open to duty in the morning, bring your duty before Him in prayer, and resolve with His help to do your duty well. In your more speculative moments, when your thoughts take a larger range, bring your conscience still to Him, and consider this question chiefly, "What is God showing me to be true and right ?" This will be to you a sustaining power to bear you above despondency and keep your aim true and your energies vigorous. And by so doing you will serve that service which is perfect freedom, and further that reign under which is no bondage, the reign of human and Christian excellence, which is the reflexion of the Divine perfection, to bring about which Christ died, to ensure which he reigns for ever.

IV

Election and Privilege in Religion.

IV.

Election and Privilege in Religion.

(Preached before the University of Oxford, November 2, 1879.)

"That we should be a kind of first-fruits of His creatures."—
JAMES i. 18.

AMONG the antagonisms which it is the function
of Christianity to destroy, and which I have made it
the special object of my sermons here to attempt to
abate, there is none deeper than that which springs
from religious privilege. It is impossible to deny
that religious privilege exists. Men are not placed
on an absolute equality. There have been chosen
nations, and there are chosen souls, such as those
whose memory was celebrated in yesterday's festival
of All Saints. The Christian Church is chosen from
the rest of mankind. The clergy have a pre-eminence within the Church. There are individuals who
through special advantages or special endowments
attain an eminence which those differently placed
cannot possibly attain. And the assertion of this
has at times had the effect of filling the possessors
of religious privilege with pride and contempt of
others, while it has aroused in those less privileged a
sense of injustice, a bitter resentment, and a rebellion

against the Divine decree.   Where is the charm
which will exorcise these evils and vindicate the
ways of God to man, and turn the galling sense of
inequality into that in which we can rest content—a
diversity of endowment for a common service ?   It
is to be found in the belief consciously held and
worked out, that the purpose for which we are called
is not to be select and separate, but to serve others, not
to be a peculiar treasure in the sense in which the
Jews were apt to apply these words to themselves,
but the first-fruits of God's creatures ; that the end of
election is not our personal happiness, nor even our
personal holiness, but that we may be the channels of
good to mankind.

Let us set before ourselves the antagonism which
we desire to abate.   We are Christians and believe
that Christianity contains the saving truth for individuals and mankind ; but this may so be asserted
as to breed mere self-complacency in us.   It is said
that the old British Church did nothing to evangelise
the Saxons because the possession of Christianity was
the peculiar treasure which gave them the pre-eminence
over their adversaries.   It is said that the Boers of
South Africa, who pride themselves in their possession of the Bible, have used this pre-eminence to
encourage in themselves a destructive and mur-
derous contempt for the heathen around them.   A
similar spirit often lurks unexpressed amongst others
than the Boers who boast of the Christian name.
Again, Christianity springs from Judaism, and " Sal-

vation is of the Jews." But He who spoke these
words had nothing more constantly at heart than
to do away with the enmity founded on the religious
privilege of the Jews, an enmity so deep that to St.
Paul the abatement of it was the grand mystery of
the Gospel. And in our own day the assertion of the
Jewish revelation has often been used to dim the sense
of 'God's universal Fatherhood, and consequently of
man's universal brotherhood. The assertion, again,
of the divine nature of our Lord is often the cause
of stumbling, because it seems that it draws away
the divine from all else, and absorbs into itself the
vital sap of the Divine Spirit which should quicken
the rest of the race and its leaders. So, too, the
position and privileges of the ordained ministers of
Christ may be so asserted as to make them the exclusive channels of grace, and to close up all other
channels of divine influence : and both at home, and
still more abroad, the alienation of clergy and laity
becomes a source of disquiet and of hatred. And in
the individual life, and that of religious societies, can
we say that Pharisaism and self-righteousness are
dead ? Is it not rather the tendency of every
religious movement to separate its sincerest votaries from their fellows, to make them into a coterie
in which their own privileges become exclusive, and
their own peculiarities the essence of religion, and
injustice is done to the convictions and spiritual
position of others ? We might multiply examples ;
but enough has been said to place the evil clearly

before us.   How can it be combated and eradicated ?

It is of no use to deny religious privilege, for it
exists.   To deny the pre-eminence of Christianity, or
the divinity of Christ, to make the religion of Israel
merely one of many religions holding an equal rank
in the education of the race, to deny the principle of
ministerial power in the Church or the eminence of
individual elect natures, is contrary to fact and to
experience.   Such an attempt to introduce a levelling
. democracy into spiritual affairs, is, in that sphere, as
in politics, merely the reaction from the overstrain of
the autocratic or hierarchical principle.   It is not the
fact that we are all alike in capacity, or disposition,
or opportunity.   What we have to do is to accept the
existence of these distinctions, to admit that religious
privilege is a fact, to estimate its meaning, bearing,
and circumference, by the guiding light of a conviction of God's love and His redemptive purpose ;
but on the other hand to be aware of the danger
and abuse to which this principle is liable, and to
shew that the true religious privilege is simply the
opportunity of doing good, the means of ensuring the
ingathering of the harvest of which it is the first-fruits.
We may then make such applications of this principle
as will duly test and enforce it.

I.—It may be said that religious privilege is the
result of man's own choice.   This man chose to
school himself to duty, or usefulness, or the discharge of special functions, and another did not.

The former enjoys the distinction of a pre-eminence in godliness and usefulness; and it is his own doing. But this will not account for all cases. Even in the case supposed, who gave this man the force of will or the power of perception which enabled him to gain this pre-eminence? And in a great many cases our own choice has little to do with the matter. No one would maintain that by any effort of choice or will a Hindoo who had never heard of Christianity could become a Christian. All the great leaders of Israel confessed that it was not to their own doing that their high position was due, but to God's sovereign choice. We see a man who has gained a position of extraordinary influence, and we ask how this has come about. We see others who had equal abilities, equal goodness, equal energy, who yet have never taken a similar position. Whatever place we allow to men's power of choice and will, we must ultimately fall back on the "Providence which shapes our ends, rough hew them how we will."

I do not purpose, as you may well believe, to embark upon the question of free will and the divine sovereignty. But I may point out that it is by no means necessary to embrace either term in an absolute way. We should be false to our consciousness were we to deny that we have a certain power over our own destiny and over the formation of our own character, and that for this we may be judged by the ordinary rules of human responsibility. But in these rules there is nothing absolute; our free will is strictly limited in its scope and in its issue. We should' be false to our still deeper consciousness as well as to the whole tenour of observed facts were we to deny that we are encompassed by a power far beyond our own control, to whom we owe our being, our character, our position in the world, and the good or evil fortune (for so we must necessarily term it) which forms an integral part of the conditions of our lives. What can we do but confess this and take some other road than that of an assumed equality of advantage in thinking aright of the ways of God towards us?

Whether or not there be anything absolute in the appellation of Father by which we know God, it is certainly the truest and most suggestive name which has been given to Him ; and the hypothesis which it presents (if it be no more) tends more than any other to solve the riddle of the world. In a family you constantly see that the good influence of the father gives a character to the whole society, and that this character communicates itself insensibly to the younger members of the family. Each one, no doubt, has his separate character, and shows this at times, not only by a difference of disposition, but by wilfulness, or rebellion, or neglect, or breaking away from the family customs. But the father's influence is a constant, pressing power, which for the most part overcomes the resistance ; and the family type of character is preserved, not without modification, not in equal degrees, yet so that the designs of the head of the family are in the end and in the main accom-

plished. What we see in the family we may see in
the world at large, of which God is the Father.
There is a certain limited scope for the exercise of
human will, but the force which we interpret as
the will of the Father is ever there ; it compels us
by the stress of outward circumstances, by the limita-
tions imposed by climate or the narrowness of means,
or the defect of bodily or mental strength, or by
some turn in the path of life which brings a neglected
truth irresistibly to view ; it is reflected upon us
by the thoughts of our minds and by the experience
of our fellows ; it is constantly present in a Christian education to those on whom the true light
shines ; it never ceases, so that we may sometimes
see a return towards God even in the worst men at
the latest hour. All this is best expressed by the
image (if it be no more) of a father watching over
his family and training them for the possession of his
own character. There is a space for choice and will,
but a much wider field for fatherly influence, which
eventually, and, as we cannot but hope, universally
will carry all before it.

We cannot avoid attributing the difference of
religious privilege to God. But this does not throw
us back on the notion of an arbitrary choice which
condemns some of its offspring to eternal misery and
sin, while it exalts others to the position of favourites.
We are coming to perceive the universal love of God,
and to believe that it will have universal success at
the last. We acknowledge, moreover, that religious

privilege is of many kinds, that it sometimes is reversed in the course of life, that men must be judged according to their works, that the last are first and the first last. When we have made these admissions, what remains of religious privilege is a certain pre-eminence, like that of the elder brother in a family, where all are treated impartially, and all work for each other's good.

That this pre-eminence exists it would be useless to deny. Indeed, we may say more. It seems to be a necessary part of the construction of human society. It has analogies in every department of human life. We commonly say that religion came to us through the Jews, art and intellectual thought through the Greeks, law through the Romans, family life through the Germans. Each of these implies a position of privilege or pre-eminence in the nations who have thus been' the channel of good to men. And, similarly, every invention has come to us through a specially gifted and privileged inventor. Every great movement in social or political life may be traced to some individual or some set of men, who have been privileged to be its originators. The diffusion of truth is not by the equal instruction of all men at the same moment, but by rings and circles of influence, to which the privilege is given of recognising the truth, and through whom it spreads and spreads till it becomes the possession of all. Why should it be different with religious truth and goodness? And if not, then the doctrine of election and of spiritual privilege is only according to the general law by which the existence of men in society is ruled.

But it may be asked whether this fact does not militate against the justice of God in the same way as the old doctrine of election and reprobation. Is it not a mere modification of that doctrine when we say that some enjoy a special privilege which to others is denied? We can hardly say this, unless our idea of justice demands a formal and exact equality, or even uniformity, in the construction of the world. Every variety implies in some sense superiority or inferiority. But who would wish for a mere uniformity, which would be the destruction of all that is interesting, of all that is beautiful, of all emulation, of all excellence? Who cannot see that to receive from one another and to impart to each other what we mutually lack, to win our way to whatever good we are capable of through conflict and aspiration, is a nobler thing than, on an exact level, to be the recipients of an exact equality of advantages? Why should we envy those who have endowments above our own, or despise those who have less? From the one let us gladly receive, to the others let us gladly impart.

Though we cannot deny the existence of religious privilege, we may take from it all that is invidious, and all that causes division, by pointing out that the true religious privilege is to be pre-eminent in serving others. The people of Israel, who are the type of the possessors of religious privilege, were chosen, not for

I

themselves, but that they might do good to mankind.
Their conflicts, their very aberrations, were the means
whereby they fulfilled God's purpose. The servant
of the Lord was often blind and deaf, but he taught
others still. And the loudest blame of the Old
Testament and the New is directed against religious
privilege when it assumes the form of selfishness, and
congratulates itself on its superiority. Then it ceases
to be privilege, and becomes the means, first of pride,
and then of falling. It is possible that the analogy
of the arts here fails us, for the elect of sculpture or
of painting may, perhaps, have his satisfaction to
himself; but the more nearly we approach to things
human and divine, the more we find that no excellence or pre-eminence can exist except under the
condition of imparting its best to others. The poet
may be lonely, but his aliment is the sympathy of his
kind. The discoverer in science or in medicine is
fired by the benefit he may bestow on others, and the
value of his discovery is to be measured by the power
which it has of being communicated. Religious
privilege, we may be sure, whether in the teaching or
the life, is nullified by the touch and taint of selfishness. It is valid just so far as it serves the interests, and
as it becomes the heritage, of mankind. So long, indeed,
as men think of God's redeeming mercy as princi-
pally occupied in saving us from a penalty and
giving us happiness, election will still mean to them
an invidious preference in the distribution of favours.
But once let it become the settled conviction in our

own minds and in our preaching, that its object is that expressed in the words, " That we may be partakers of the divine nature," and this notion of an invidious preference vanishes. For the divine nature is that of unceasing, active, self-imparting love, which works and suffers to save us. And the partaking of this nature, the communion with God, shows itself in self-sacrifice for truth and right. What is there of invidious privilege in being called to be a leader in love, in sacrifice, or in suffering? But such leadership is the only one known to Christianity. There may have been amongst those elect natures whose memory in these two days of All Saints and All Souls is dear to Christian hearts, some who have had less of the practical power which draws men to right, and whose life was spent in meditation. But it was always acknowledged that even the lives most abstracted from the world were spent for the world's benefit; and the placing of All Souls' Day after All Saints' associated with the blissful servants and martyrs of Christ those unperfected natures who were yet, through suffering, purging away their mortal taint. This was but the superstitious form of a true conviction, the conviction that the very essence of saintliness is to be self-imparting. We can recognise more than could the men of the dark ages that the truly saintly life is not one spent in an effort to escape from or mitigate the punishments of another world, but one spent rejoicingly in the present service of God and man. But in all ages of the Church the

I 2

divine nature has been recognised as the giving up
of self for the good of men. We value the saintly
recluse so far as his mortification and absorption in
God are genuine, and so far as his prayers are for the
good of mankind. Otherwise, when we have a suspicion that an element which is unreal and selfish is
present, we can hardly repress our scorn. The men
who have lived for their kind, who have had the least
consciousness of mere privilege, who have aspired
(and aspiration implies a humbling sense of imper-
fection), these are the true elect, the possessors of
spiritual privilege, a privilege which, in various
degrees, may become the possession of all.

II.—We must apply and illustrate our principle
so as to test and enforce it.

1. I begin with that which occupies the chief
place in practical life and in Christian theology, the
call or appointment of Christ to be the head of all—
"That in all things," to use the words of St. Paul,
"He might have the pre-eminence." He is the elect
of the elect. In Him all other election has its rise
and validity. We are not here engaged with the
metaphysical questions relating to His pre-existence,
or His relationship to the Godhead apart from
humanity, but with the practical doctrine of His
pre-eminence over all mankind, and over all created
things. Is it not clear that it was a pre-eminence in
service, in devotion to the good of mankind? St.
Paul speaks of his being in the form of God only to
heighten the sense of His voluntary self-abasement.

He thought it not robbery to be equal with God—
that is, He did not grasp at that position as a selfish
advantage; but He made Himself of no reputation,
He emptied Himself. These words are but an echo
of those in which He Himself described His pre-
eminence. "Let the chief be he that serves, as the
Son of Man came not to be ministered unto, but to
minister, and to give His life a ransom for many."
How can the position of one who spoke thus of
Himself have become the subject of contention
among His followers, or the occasion of stumbling to
those without, except by a misunderstanding of His
claims, a misunderstanding also of the divine nature
which His character revealed? Do not all confess
Him to be the truest servant and benefactor of
mankind? Is not the conception of God which He
presents—that, namely, of a righteous Father, who is
incessantly working for our good—one which irresistibly commends itself to all who have pondered on
His life and death? Why should we ban those who,
under whatever name, accept Him as morally and
practically supreme, to whom His word is law, who
desire only to live in the spirit of His life? And how
can that claim be the subject of contention which is a
claim only to a supremacy of self-devotion, a leadership in the sacrifice of self for God and truth, for
right, and for love to men? This is the supreme
religious privilege. Does not its very statement
command the assent of mankind?

And with this is closely connected the pre-

eminence of faith in Christ, or in God as revealed in
Christ, which is, so to speak, the elect of Christian
graces, the *articulus stantisa ut cadentis ecclesiæ*. If faith
implied, as it has often been taken to imply, an
assent to a whole *corpus theologiæ*, to articles such as
those of the Athanasian Creed, to peculiar theories of
the Atonement, to miraculous histories, the assertion of
its unique importance might well, as it has often
done, excite derision, or vehement repudiation.   But
if it be, as I have tried to point out, a sympathy
with the divine goodness which shows itself forth in
our Saviour's character, a communion of service
rendered to mankind, an aspiration which may exist
(as it did exist in prophets and righteous men of
old). in the form of a longing for a goodness unseen,
unrealised ; then I can hardly conceive how any one
can refuse to admit it, except where the selfish film
is but partially removed from the spiritual eye.   Even
in their common judgments men hardly test one
another by any other standard than that of a harmony with the spirit which inspired the life and
death of Jesus of Nazareth.

2. Let us take next the pre-eminence of the
Jewish and Christian revelations which gives so great
a privilege to their adherents.   To this privilege the
same principle must be applied.   We vindicate, not
its exclusiveness but its supremacy.   It is the first-
fruits, the prime confession of God, the pledge that
the whole harvest of the confession of God throughout the world is counted genuine, that in every nation

he that feareth God and worketh righteousness is accepted of Him. This is a day in which fresh discoveries are being made in the history of religions, and each discovery brings to light not points of difference but analogies and resemblances between these religions in their best form and Christianity itself. We are in the presence of a new science, the science of comparative religion; and men are found, strangely enough, trembling lest the comparison should diminish the claims of the religion in which they have found their life. But if the resemblances which are traced are genuine, we must welcome them as pointing to a truer and a grander claim for Christianity than that exclusiveness which has often been asserted, the claim namely of standing supreme, surrounded by supports and witnesses whose sound goes forth to the ends of the world. It is the claim to embody and complete whatever elements of truth are found in the other religions. If Greece had its heroes and demigods, what was this but a witness to the divine in humanity which is realised in Christ? If Egypt taught the divine in animal life, and Africa the divine in inanimate things, is not even this recognised when Christ is declared to be the firstborn of all the creation? If the Vedas saw God's power in Indra, the giver of rain, and Rita the universal law, Christ tells, only in a nobler sense, of the Father who makes his rain to descend on the evil and on the good, of One whose will is eternal life to His creatures. The self-sacrifice of Buddha finds its

counterpart of devotion, its outshining sun of redemptive hope, in the self-sacrifice of Christ. The rigid
monotheism and fatalism of Mahomet stands out
purified in the teaching of our Lord as the unswerving
will of righteous love. And if the Persian and Egyptian religions spoke of immortality, the Christian
presents to us as our goal an eternal persistence of a
life of purity. All religions have rendered some
service to mankind. The claim of Christ's religion is
not such as to deny, but to give validity to all those
strivings towards truth which we find in other religions.
Its claim is that it has rendered the chief service and
is still capable of rendering it. And its adherents are
the first-fruits of the harvest of the earth, not because
of outward advantages which flow from its possession,
but because and on the condition that they are occupied
in communicating to all men the blessings of which
they are the first possessors.

3. Our principle of supremacy or prerogative as
contrary to exclusiveness must be applied to Christian
leadership, and especially to the position of the
clergy. The ideal of a Christian clergy is that the
natural leaders of the congregation, those who are
shown by a natural selection to have been chosen and
endowed with special gifts for guidance and edification,
should be set apart; in other words, that the gifts of
the Spirit, their call to the work, should be recognised,
and full opportunity given them for the exercise of
those gifts. They are priests, but in a community
every one of whom is a priest; and priesthood to a

Christian means, if we follow the teaching of the Epistle to the Hebrews, self-sacrifice for the good of men. To harden this down into a formal ordinance, to look at those only as priests and ministers who are formally ordained by the imposition of episcopal hands, to make the outward position, the outward rite, the chief thing on which the spiritual life depends, is to ignore the very genius of Christianity. The external order is, indeed, necessary ; it is the ordinary channel of grace ; it is right, as a matter of discipline, that it should be maintained ; and our effort must always be to make the outward order correspond with the inward fact. But we must recognise this, that the Christian Church is not established for worship alone, and that therefore the ministry of worship can never comprehend all Christian leadership or priesthood. Whether there will ever come a time when an outward ordination will be bestowed on others than those who lead us in prayer, who preach in the congregation and administer the sacraments, I do not know ; nor can this be a very important question to those who look below the surface of things. But of this I am sure, that God has, by His Spirit, appointed many holy orders in His Church besides that of prayer and preaching, and that, whether we use the words or no, we must recognise holy orders of educators, of thinkers, of investigators of nature, of artists, of professional men, and of political guides. The order of the clergy may still be the chief among the holy orders of the Christian Commonwealth ; but it must be the first-fruits of the rest, not the exclusive depository of grace. It must hold its pre-eminence on the condition of self-sacrifice, and of imbuing the other orders with the spirit which it has been the first to receive. And in the supreme work of prayer and instruction (for it will always be supreme), our effort, as clergymen, should be, not to keep as much as possible in our own hands, but to diffuse the gifts of edification as widely as possible. There is no likelihood—we may well wish that there were—of our services being no longer needed through Christian knowledge being universally diffused, and every society of men being bound together by prayer. But the ideal promise of prophecy is, " They shall not teach every man his neighbour, saying know the Lord, for all shall know me ;" and this ideal should be aimed at now by drawing out all spiritual capacities, and associating with us as many as the exigencies of external order will admit. And above all, we should be anxious that all who lead and teach should do so in the spirit of self-sacrifice, which is, let me repeat, the only true priesthood—the spirit which refuses to separate itself from mankind, and to become a spirit of clique, the spirit which longs to share all the good which it contains at whatever cost to itself with the widest possible circle.

4. And lastly, the principle of supremacy as against exclusiveness is to be applied to the position of religious men. To some it seems invidious and even untrue to speak of any as specially religious

men. But the fact that some men are specially
religious can hardly be denied. Indeed, this has
appeared to some so evident, and to involve so great
a distinction, that they have held that some are called
to be religious men, while on the rest no obligation
rests to think of religion, since they have no capacity
for it. And one distinguished writer, vexed with the
phases of faith through which he had passed, has
contended that there are some spiritual natures who
might be called twice born, while the rest must be
content with some attainment of a more earthly
virtue. Between these extremes lies the truth. When
personal religion is deeply felt, it seems at first to
separate a man from others. No one, he almost
inclines to say, has ever seen things as I see, or felt
as I feel. What a new view of the world is opened
to him! What discoveries of the great distinction
of evil and good! What a light, revealing, like a
flash of lightning, all the moral world which before
was dim in its proper colours! What a sense of God's
mercy in Christ! What a longing for holiness, like
the first consciousness of a deep human affection!
What a sense of responsibility, and of the vast issues
of eternal life and death! What is this but being
separated, and called by the grace of God? And can
you believe that all alike are thus separated? It is
not so. You find some few who have felt with you.
You dimly suspect that there are others. But beyond
these the world still seems to lie in the outer darkness.
But neither is that quite the case. There is a spiritual

nature as well as a moral in which all the world are
kin. The words and deeds in which it is expressed,
if only they bear the impress of true love, will not fail
to meet with a response. Often has that occurred
which is related of himself by a great soldier, whose
rough appearance seemed very unsympathetic to a
lady who gave him a book of devotion :—" She evi-
dently imagined," so he writes in his journal, " that
men like me have no thought of such things. But we
have." And many passages in the journal of that
great man tell of his consciousness of the great
struggle, as he terms it, between the evil spirit and
the good all through the world, and of the paramount
importance of allying ourselves with the good spirit.
There is no absolute line of separation to be traced.
The religious man has a vast pre-eminence in religion ;
but he need not think that others are wholly destitute
of it. Least of all need he sit passive until by some
convulsion of nature the hearts of men are changed.
If his religion be true, it will show itself, not only or
chiefly in those good qualities which make him
different from others, but in those which are simplest,
most obvious, most universal. His image is not that
of a Galahad urged by an ecstacy of devotion to
pursue the Holy Grail till he is lost to human sight
in regions where men cannot follow, but an Arthur
surrounded by valiant men, redressing human
wrong, and leading the way into the better land of
righteousness.

And this is true also in reference to the diversities

of religious opinion or culture which to some men are so great a stumbling-block, and which have often been so dealt with that they have hindered the progress of true religion. Some have viewed these differences as fundamental, and, taking sides in the conflict engendered by them, have made all religion to turn on the points of difference ; while others have regarded the points of difference as so entirely un-essential that they would obliterate them, and leave to us only the pale and peaceful image of a colourless religion. The principle I have advocated to-day solves the difficulty. Each opinion, or sect, or school, or church, if we look at it impartially, has at least some element of good in it. Its distinguishing feature is, at least in its origin, an inspiration, a reve-lation of truth in some new aspect, to be dealt with not only with tenderness, but with reverence, in the spirit of the words " Quench not the Spirit." But, if it is to be fruitful, it must communicate itself, and that not only to the first nucleus of specially called disciples ; it must show its capacity of harmonising with and inspiring the life of mankind.

A great responsibility rests upon those who are introducing any new aspect of truth to the notice of their contemporaries. Let it be granted that the truth they have before them is pure and absolute, that the discovery and assertion of it is their special privilege and high endowment ; yet it must not be so asserted as to throw blame on the whole life of the generation in which it emerges, or to grow into

exaggerations which make it hardly recognisable, or
to dwarf the proportions of all other aspects of truth,
or to form its adherents into a narrow coterie, speaking a language unintelligible to their brethren.   The
possessors of truth must hold it under this condition
—that they make it intelligible, communicable ; that
their thoughts range in sympathy with their kind.
They are, in respect of their own way of thinking, a
kind of first-fruits.   They are not to enter into a
closed room, and take the key from the door, while
they sit with their friends at the banquet of truth,
and mock at or sigh over the vulgar herd outside.
The mysteries of the Gospel are free to all mankind.
The door must be left wide open, and those within
must issue forth and welcome all to share their treasure.   They must not reach their point by overbear-
ing others or taking from them the truths, distorted
though they may be, on which till then they have
been leaning ; nor must they expect that the task of
convincing the world will be performed easily and
quickly by a few valiant words.   But they may hope
that after a life of toil they may have the proud
consciousness that they have added to the sum of
true conviction, that they have been helpers of the
angels of God's mercy and truth in gathering in
the harvest of the earth.

What we need is a religion which will reconcile,
not divide; which will introduce a divine harmony
where hitherto there has been separation.   I quote
here words which are not less needed now than when

they were first published by one amongst us twenty-four years ago :—" The God of peace rest upon you, is the concluding benediction of most of the Epistles. How can he rest upon us, who draw so many hard lines of demarcation between ourselves and other men, who oppose the Church and the world, Sundays and working days, revelation and science, the past and the present, the life and state of which religion speaks, and the life which we ordinarily lead ? . . . If in the age of the Apostle it seemed to be the duty of the believers to separate themselves from the world and take up a hostile position, not less marked in the present age is the duty of abolishing in a Christian country what has now become an artificial distinction, and seeking by every means in our power, by fairness, by truthfulness, by knowledge, by love unfeigned, by the absence of party and prejudice, by acknowledging the good in all things, to reconcile the Church to the world, the one half of our nature to the other ; drawing the mind off from speculative difficulties, or matters of party and opinion, to that which all equally acknowledge, and almost equally fall short of —the life of Christ."

I only add to these eloquent words, the aim of which must be unreservedly accepted, that the consummation to which they point cannot be attained merely by ignoring the differences or distinctions which have divided men ; but by giving to these distinctions their legitimate place. That place is not to be absolute, or supreme, or enduring, but to be the means of impressing upon the whole community some aspect of truth or goodness which they would otherwise be tempted to forget. The Sunday is taken as the first-fruits of the week, in order that it may breathe the rest of God upon the world,

> " Till all both rest day and employ,
>   Be one Lord's day of holy joy."

The Church is called as an elect body, in order that through it the whole world may become the kingdom of God. The priesthood or ministry is to be the means by which all are to become priests and ministers through the diffusion of self-sacrifice throughout the whole community. Let us so use whatever privilege or pre-eminence, whatever distinctions of character, of culture, of discernment, of faith we may possess, not so as to emphasise or perpetuate such distinctions, but so that whatever is good in them may become the universal inheritance, that the Christianity of our day may be the first-fruits of a world which we are fellow-workers with God in bringing back to Himself, through Jesus Christ our Lord.

V

Critical Thought and Practical Ministry.

Critical Thought and Practical Ministry.

(Preached before the University of Oxford, May 30, 1880.)

"Vanity of vanities, saith the preacher, all is vanity. And moreover, because the preacher was wise, he still taught the people knowledge ; yea, he gave good heed, and sought out, and set in order many proverbs. The preacher sought to find out acceptable words : and that which was written was upright, even words of truth."—ECCLES. xii. 8, 9, 10.

I WISH in this sermon to draw a lesson from the Book of Ecclesiastes which is not very commonly drawn — namely, the connection between critical thought and practical ministry. I need not point out that the Book of Ecclesiastes is tinged with critical thought in almost every sentence. It has been called, not wrongly, a sceptical book. The temper of the writer is not that of the man who trusts, who readily gives himself, but of one who examines, who looks narrowly at each idea, each project ; one whose monotonous refrain borders on despair: "Vanity of vanities, all is vanity." It has often been observed that this despair is not final; men have pointed to the words, "Let us hear the conclusion of the whole matter, Fear God and keep his commandments, for

J 2

this is the whole duty of man." · They have, perhaps,
gone as far as to note the kind of approval which the
writer gives, still in a semi-sceptical vein, to a calm
and hopeful beneficence. "Cast thy bread upon the
waters and thou shalt find it after many days." But
what has rarely been dwelt upon is the effort evi-
dently made by the preacher in this last chapter to
show that he is speaking neither at hazard, nor only
in gloomy monologue, but that he has a distinct purpose of edification in what he says. He insists that
with all his sceptical thought he yet is a preacher, one
who seeks to do men good by the use of earnest
words ; he declares that all his life long he was
occupying himself in teaching the people knowledge,
and that he did this strenuously, continuously ; and,
moreover, that he did not fling out his doubts with a
view to distress men, or in a way which might alienate
them from the truth, but that he sought acceptable
words, that which was honest indeed and upright, but
that which, at the same time, would convey the truth
sympathetically and congenially to his hearers. The
teaching which this passage suggests to us is this—
that critical thought is not necessarily unsympathetic
or forbidding, but that it has a real affinity with
those purposes of edification for which the ministry of
souls exists. We are apt to represent to ourselves this
critical thought as a dangerous being without a conscience. We talk of a remorseless criticism, of cold
and colourless reason, of negative theology. We con-
jure up the chilling spectre of a system or a spirit

which, careless of the pain which it inflicts, cuts up by
the roots the fair, fond flowers of hope, makes sentiment ridiculous and aspiration illusory, trips up each
effort before it has fairly started, and stunts all generous enterprise. That there is such critical thought as
this cannot be denied; it may be that some men even
feel a cruel pleasure in the pain they inflict by its
exercise, just as some persons delight in scenting
heresy in the works of conscientious and earnest men.
But the abuse of criticism does not hinder its legitimate use. Every faculty may be misused or may be
pressed to so extreme a point as to become dangerous, destructive, and self-stultifying. But criticism has
its proper place. What is it but the expression of
reason and of truth? How can it interfere with efforts
to do good? If there is anything false, or one-sided,
or impracticable in such efforts, must it not be a
benefit to them to be corrected? If they contain an
element which is illusory, is it not necessary that the
illusions should gradually be brought to light? How
can an army advance without danger if it has no in-
telligence department? When the last word of criticism has been spoken, it still remains true that the
object of life is love, and that the highest duty of man
during the span of his existence on earth is to minister to his fellows, and add to the sum of truth and
goodness among them; and it also remains true that,
in seeking these things, faith and hope are his stimulus
and his guide.

I purpose to discuss this first in general, and

secondly in reference to the practical wants of the present day.

I.—It is sometimes accepted as an axiom, and that not by one side alone, that a theology which contains much of negation tends to become no theology at all; that if you begin to touch the fabric of existing beliefs, and to say, this is exaggerated, this is not scriptural, this is expressed too strongly, this is not so certain as you imagine, you are really meaning to break down the whole fabric. An uncomfortable feeling of uncertainty is aroused, and men begin to feel as if all that was precious was being torn from them. But, you say, "All that I am telling you is true. Do you not admit that my criticisms are just?" When men are thus driven, they are inclined to reply, "We cannot be troubled with arguments; we want to do good, to enjoy our religion, to preserve the fabric of our belief and 'our life intact." Thus we have an antagonism set up between the spirit of criticism and the spirit of practical good. And this putting aside of pious and practical aims is often accepted as necessary by men of critical minds: or, if they see the value of practical good, they hold their critical faculties in one hand and their piety in the other, so that the two do not come near each other. There is a saying of a great critic of the origins of Christianity, that criticism founds nothing, that fanaticism alone is creative. If that were true, we might well say, as that same writer has said with reference to another subject, that God and nature had deceived us : for what deception could be so great as that our deepest affection should urge us on a path which truthful criticism would show to be wrong? We may be sure that Christianity, the mother of all reconciliation, contains within its capacious bosom the connecting principle which will allay this apparent antagonism, an antagonism which, if it be not allayed, can hardly prove anything short of deadly.

It is not true that a negative theology is merely and simply negative. Not only do the widest negations ever made by sane men leave room still for the life of love and goodness to spring up, but many negations are requisite in every age in order to bring into due prominence the central truth on which such a life is founded. If it be the fact that something of fanaticism has often been mixed with the founding of great institutions, it is also the fact that what the fanatical element has built requires to be pulled down again and rebuilt upon a more solid foundation. And it may be said with truth that the greatest founders have been also the greatest destroyers. You must clear away the rubbish before you can begin to build. Let us draw out these propositions somewhat more fully.

1. There is an impression which is very commonly countenanced in religious teaching, that there is more danger from the negation of truth than from the affirmation of error ; at least, that to detract from truth is a much more dangerous thing than to exaggerate it. It is a great mistake to compare two

processes equally false, and to give the preference to
one over the other. Yet this is what we are constantly tempted to do. We take some extreme,
exaggerated system, and say, "At least in this the
truth is confessed, while those who resist it are
denying the truth altogether." But it is at least
doubtful whether it is worse to deny the truth
altogether than to affirm it in a form which by
exaggeration perverts it. To take an extreme case,
which may bring into relief what it is here sought
to enforce. Suppose yourself to have been living
amongst the worshippers of Moloch, and suppose
one bold man to have arisen and maintained that
there is no God ; you would hardly have thought
it right to assert that it was better to hold with the
worshippers of Moloch, because they confessed a God,
though a monstrous one. You would feel that in all
probability the man who under such circumstances
had the courage to call himself an Atheist was a
better man than the votaries of a God of cruelty ;
and you would remain of this opinion, notwith-
standing that it might be pointed out that the
worshippers of Moloch were supported by the
enthusiasm of a united people, and that their
enthusiastic belief was accompanied by self-devotion
and eager convictions, and the readiness to endure
as well as to inflict pain, and the building of magnificent temples, and the collection of vast multitudes
at their religious rites. You would say, "The
affirmation of a cruel God is false and hateful ;

and he that denies the divine altogether cannot be more false." The most extreme negation is really the correction, often the needful correction, of the extreme and untruthful affirmation.

What we have to deal with is, of course, a much more subtle thing than this. But the principle still holds, that exaggeration mars truth as much as does negation. When superstitions grow up beside a truth, they are like the parasitical growths of the forests of South America, which appear to be parts of the trees to which they cling, but encircle them and overtop them, and in the end strangle them. It is not true that you can have an important truth mixed up with superstitions, and yet unimpaired. The superstitions come to be looked upon as of equal value with the truth, and the result is that first the truth is degraded to the level of the superstitions, and then the superstitions become everything, and the truth well nigh disappears. When a negative criticism comes in on a scene like this, and argues or laughs away the superstitions, it seems, no doubt, as if nothing were left. The Anthropomorphist monk of the Egyptian desert, when he was told that the Church of Alexandria had affirmed that we could think of God otherwise than as having hands and feet, exclaimed, "You have taken away, you have destroyed my God." But in truth the negation is a liberating process, and when criticism has done its work, there is room, which there was not before, for the truth to arise and grow. The greatest negations have commonly had an affirmation which they presupposed; and movements, like that of Protestantism, which have a negative name, have really been the reassertion of great principles. The old question, "Where was your Church before Luther?" might be met with another, "Where were truth, and goodness, and living faith, in the Church of the 16th century, till Luther arose to revive and disengage them?"

But it is said with truth that a certain superstition, or extra belief, is often a kind of natural integument of faith; that there are illusions which are really educational; that the husk and the rind are necessary to the growth of the fruit. We may well admit this as true; but it makes the demand for criticism all the more pressing. For that which is merely educational is meant to pass away, the illusion must give place to the reality. Men are apt to cling to the past, and make much of the form after it has ceased to be real; and the function of criticism is to point this out, to help the natural process by which the reason and conscience of mankind by degrees emerge from their childish integuments.

And even where negation seems barest, you may often see that it is really directed against the integument which ought to pass away, not against the truth which is destined to remain. There are many who seem to be Atheists, while what they are really denying is not the existence of God but a peculiar presumption as to the mode of His existence. There is a kind of mechanical conception of the operation of the Deity, on which all religion is apt to be staked, the conception of a God who interferes from without with the orderly evolution of nature and humanity. " I see no trace of such interference," says the man of science ; "such a God as this is abhorrent to all our experience." He seems to be denying God. What he is really doing is to clear the way for a truer and more living conception of the Divine operations, the conception of a God who is immanent in His creatures, and who works, in some manner beyond the measure of our thoughts, in and through nature and mankind.

It is true, again, that there are accompaniments of faith which are harmless, perhaps indispensable. But the danger is a real one that these accompaniments come to be placed on an equality with faith and virtue, and that, when this comes to pass, the accompaniments are apt to remain in full vigour while faith and virtue take the second place, and at last are ignored. Our Lord pronounced a woe upon those who, by tithing mint and anise and cumin, had come to neglect the weightier matters of the law. He did not indeed forbid these smaller observances, but He denied them any place at all in comparison with judgment and mercy and the love of God. And the voice of God Himself is as often heard in negation as in affirmation. The commandments are almost all negations. Thou shalt have none other God beside me. Thou shalt worship no graven image. These are the great negations of God, and from under their indispensable protest comes forth the great affirmation,—Thou shalt love the Lord thy God with all thy heart.

2. Now, examine for a moment the statement which is supposed to be historical—that critical thought founds nothing, that fanaticism is needed for all construction. Contrast with it that which has been said above, that what has been built by fanaticism requires to be taken down and reconstructed.

Take the example of Mahometanism, which has been one of the most stupendous creations of a fanatical impulse that the world has even seen. There was indeed an original truth at its base, the assertion of the one supreme God alike against heathen and Christian idolatry : but side by side with this grew up the fabric of the all-conquering empire of the Caliphs, of a sensual paradise, of a ritual which, if not so complex as those of some parts of Christendom, is much more binding and more superstitious, and of a system of laws which, though but partially moral, are all incorporated into the Divine. Does any one now believe that this system can last, or that it enshrines any principle of permanent benefit to mankind ? If some men cherish the hope that it may be reformed, the fanaticism which pushed it forward is the precise thing which prevents the fulfilment of their hopes ; for a system which professes itself to be divine in all its details must remain irreformable. And Mahometanism is becoming a curse to all who lie under its baneful shade ; a thing which is fast growing impossible, and is doomed.

Take as another example the ascetic tendency which developed itself in the Christian Church from the fourth century onwards. It is said that it was a needful protest against the immorality of the Roman world. If it had been only that, its leaders would have distinguished, like St. Paul, between the present distress and the natural order of God's providence. But they made no such distinction. They built upon the fanatical belief that family life was an evil, or at least an inferior state, that the common order of the world must be given over to Satan, that all the joy, and beauty, and refinement of life must be under a ban ; and what they built had from the first quite as much in it of curse as of blessing ; it was the parent of mis-understandings and corruptions from which religion is, even now, but slowly emerging ; and in process of time it has become almost wholly mischievous. The fanatical element, so far from being the strength of Christian monasticism, has been that which prevented its doing good, and has ensured its destruction.

You may see the same thing in respect of the fanatical exaggerations of more modern times. In the revolutionary mania in France, in 1793, some-thing, no doubt, was founded—a system of forced equality, combined with a hatred of all that bore the stamp of the *ancien régime*. But the fanaticism by which this system was supported was not its strength, but the cause of its ruin. It urged it into cruelty, into public Atheism, into the violence of the Jacobin and the Sans-culotte ; and when the reaction swiftly came, there was great danger lest even the more valuable products of the Revolution should be lost. Or take the reactionary mania which followed the wars of the Revolution, and was expressed in men like Metternich. Metternich had a system which for some fifteen years dominated Europe, and which he believed to be divine and permanent. But it was a fanatical travesty of that spirit of godly order which it pretended to represent. Was this fanaticism the means of building up a permanent home for that godly order? On the contrary, his system fell to pieces even during the lifetime of its author, and so far as it endured, was an incessant provocative to revolution, in which all that he held dear was endangered.

It may be true that mankind has hitherto advanced by means of antagonisms and fanatical exaggerations which have clashed with each other and, like forces pulling slantwise from different sides, have drawn on the central mass. We must not be hard upon the past; we may say "The times of that ignorance God winked at." But the time is come when we must attend to the real progress of mankind, and discountenance the fanatical exaggerations which the past has bequeathed to us. The place of critical thought must be re-asserted. There is a power in moderation, and truth, and equity, which the world is only now beginning to recognise. There is a reasonable religion which eschews exaggeration, and which is none the less the parent of a sober and earnest piety. There is a faculty which is certainly not the least Christ-like of our powers, which looks at both sides of a matter, which puts aside what is extreme and absurd, and acknowledges that, beyond all disputed questions, the purifying and ennobling of human life by the Spirit of Christ remains as the great object of our efforts. Will it be said that Christ was a fanatic? Will it be said that even St. Paul was one? It is surely astonishing to find that there are critics who still look upon St. Paul as a one-sided partisan. Is it not he who said "Circumcision is nothing, and uncircumcision is nothing, but faith that worketh by love?" Is it not he who urged "Let your moderation be known unto all men?" The Christian Church is the greatest of human institutions. What student of its origin can say that it owes its birth to fanaticism?

3. But here we touch the kernel of the question. In our Lord Himself we may venture to say, with perfect reverence, that we find in its purest form the combination we are seeking of critical thought with pastoral activity. He was not indifferent or over-mild. He did not accept things as they were. His energy was spent not on promoting a pietistic acquiescence, but in the criticism of existing institutions. He came to revolutionise the world. He cast a seed amongst mankind which He knew would in its growth produce enormous changes. And He set about these changes with what we need not scruple to call a

destructive vehemence. The uplifted scourge in the
hand of the Saviour expressed a true part of His
character. The invectives against the Pharisees
swept away a whole system of life with their scathing
criticism. And those who from a Pharisaic point of
view looked upon his teaching would see in it something even more negative than this. In all His
teaching on morals and religion there was not one
word about the obligation of the ceremonial law, or
the temple services, or the meetings in the syna-
gogues, with which the Jewish religion was bound up.
All this was simply ignored, and ignoring by a
winning and influential teacher is the surest form of
condemnation. It is, to use the phrase of Roman
law, the antiquation of that which is put aside. It
was this, no doubt, more than anything else, which
influenced the Pharisees to destroy Him. And then
came St. Paul, more trenchant and pointed in his
negativism, saying expressly that circumcision and
the law in its widest sense were absolutely indifferent;
and not only so, but that they might become, if more
adhered to them, the very source of evil: " The
strength of sin is the law." If we place ourselves in
the position of Jews of the first century, we can
imagine how St. Paul seemed to them a violent revo-
lutionist. As such he appeared to the Judaizing
author of the Clementines. And yet it is certain
that the churches of St. Paul were not founded on a
violent, one-sided negativism. We have but to refer
to the earnestness of his efforts in the cause of con-

ciliation as shown in the collection for the poor saints at Jerusalem, or in the controversy about the eating of things offered to idols, to see that the picture given in the Acts is true, and that that which St. Paul was aiming at throughout was the spiritual good of both sections of the early Church. He threw himself on the side where the weight of his influence was most needed, like a rhetorician who brings into prominence that side of the question which most needs to be impressed. But the rhetorician may still be perfectly truthful, earnest for good in every sense, while yet he applies himself specially to impress one side of it alone. And St. Paul, while vehement in his denunciation of Judaizers, was aiming as a faithful pastor at the spiritual good of all. Deeper far than any denunciation is the heart-felt desire: " I pray God that your whole body, and soul, and spirit may be preserved blameless to the coming of Christ." We may safely take our Lord and His chief Apostle as our example in the attempt to combine critical thought with practical ministry.

II.—Let us now come more to the facts of our own day, and apply what has been said to our actual needs.

In the present day critical and negative thought has become a factor with which every teacher must count. But it need cause us no alarm if only it is sincere and reasonable. We may welcome it, if it be such, as an ally in our efforts for the good of men.

Take an extreme case, that of one who calls

K

himself an Agnostic. He says, "I do not see that
we have light enough to affirm anything about God
or immortality." He points out that the arguments
on such subjects are derived from sentiment rather
than strict reasoning. He persists in leaving all the
great affirmations of the Christian creeds undecided.
We may quite admit that such a man can hardly
enter the Christian ministry, where declarations of
his faith are required of him such as will give confidence to the congregation to which he is to minister.
But he may, nevertheless, earnestly desire to act
rightly and also to do good to men. Moreover, the
Agnostic may possibly see some sides of Christian
work more clearly than many who seem more certain.
He may, from the very fact that he is unable to
assert anything distinct about another world, appreciate more fully the importance of justice and
goodness in this world. Nay, it is possible that he
may be of a genuinely humble temperament, and
may say to himself, "If it is my misfortune to be
unable to lay hold of God and immortality, I will
bear the uncertainty without murmuring; if it is my
fault, I will endeavour so to act that better light may
come to me. If there be indeed nothing beyond, still
the moral side of the Christian life is the truest
standard that I can follow. Let me, like Christ, go
about doing good." Because Christian doctrines are
not matters of scientific certainty, it does not follow
that they cannot be held as matters of faith and
hope; and Agnosticism still leaves room for faith

and hope : and it is in the region of faith and hope, not in that of ascertained fact, that our salvation is to be found. Special attention has been called of late to the *Reflections* of the Emperor Marcus Aurelius. We find in that book many thoughts of the kind I have just expressed. He makes sure of nothing ; only he assumes for the most part, with a kind of childlike hopefulness, that the Power which rules us is just and good ; and in the patient acquiescence in the dominion of that Power, whatever it may be, and whatever may be his own individual destiny, he sets to work to purge himself of lust and anger, to be humble, brave, gentle, compassionate, and to do good, —an endeavour the success of which is proved by the perfect correspondence of the history of his reign with the motives which his book reveals, and by the twenty years' happiness which his career gave to the Roman world. Let us not refuse the Agnostic who wishes to do good, but welcome him as a fellow-worker.

And are there not many who worship in our congregations who all their life are perplexed with doubts, like those expressed in the book of Ecclesiastes, who feel that the affirmations of our creeds go far beyond their convictions, and yet are attached to our worship, not by mere custom, but by a sincere longing to be good and to do good ? Shall we ban them from our communion by exacting as a preliminary condition that they must hold as unquestionable every fact narrated in the Bible or assumed

as true in our services? I cannot think that our
Lord would have made such a demand. I think He
would have said, "If you cannot follow me yet so as
to trust yourself to me in regions beyond human experience, yet if you love that justice and goodness
which are indeed the divine nature, I count you
amongst those who are of the truth, who know my
voice, and are my true subjects; come, go in and out
among my brethren; in time you shall know more
of me, and I will lead you into realms of fuller
light."

Or, once more, take the case of a Christian
minister who cannot accept the perfect certitude with
which supernatural things are sometimes assumed.
Is he to say, "Since I have some doubts from time to
time, and the heavenly things are overclouded to my
view, therefore I must give up the ministry and cease
to teach the people knowledge?" By no means.
These doubts may, if rightly dealt with, keep him
humble and watchful. Nay, they may be the witness
that he is of so truthful a disposition that he dares not
go a hair's-breadth in affirmation beyond his convictions; and he may do more by his truthfulness in
the instruction of the people than others by their
assurance. Nay more, such a man may be really
conceiving divine things in a truer way than those
who feel a fuller assurance; for these things are not
matters of exact demonstration which holds good for
all alike: they are matters rather of faith and hope,
which by patience and spiritual apprehension grow to

a moral, but never to a scientific, certainty. And in this life of patient hopefulness there are elements which may, through human sympathy, come home to men's souls more than the dogmatic confidence which so often meets us even in good men, and so often repels us.

The ministry of the Gospel is indeed one of joyful confidence, and to those who are of a hopeful disposition such a temperament as that of the Ecclesiast, or of the Apostle Thomas, appears uncongenial. But, among the many gifts, all of which have their functions in the perfect Christian body, we cannot deny a place to such temperaments as these. Let me trace out some of the benefits which the ministry may gain from them.

1. As regards efforts for the amelioration of men. The enthusiasm of Christian workers sometimes outruns moderation and prudence. It is hard for us to hear a plan which we have set our hearts upon questioned and criticised. Yet this criticism is very needful; for prudence and circumspection are Christian graces. And even if such criticism is discouraging, the discouragement may send us back to search into the principles on which our proposed action rests, and the plans we have formed: and if we resolve to go forward, the questioning process we have gone through will have tended to deepen our convictions and to mature our projects. The Book of Ecclesiastes is full of warnings to reformers. It does not say to them, the world does not need

reform ; but it bids them reflect that there are many things which are crooked and can never be set straight, so that they may not fret at the inevitable ; that he who would reform must lay his plans well and count the cost, else he will bring himself and his projects to ruin : it bids him remember that things are not always so bad as they look ; and that they will often right themselves if left alone ; above all, that, come what may, he must not redress wrong by wrong, and that the spirit of rebellion against authority must be resolutely suppressed. Who can say that such warnings are not needed, or that if listened to they will do other than conduce to the efficiency of the reformer's efforts? And who is there who knows the beneficent works of Christians in the present day who does not know also that they often fail for lack of the criticism of which we have spoken ? This criticism may serve to enlighten those who work, and to direct and concentrate efforts which would otherwise run to waste or injure those whom they are meant to benefit. The whole question of the relief of the poor, with the fields of effort lying beside it, affords a good illustration of this process. The easy benevolence which prompts the prodigal giving of out-door relief under the poor law, the impulsive kindness which gives to beggars in the streets and to the poor in their homes without reflecting on the moral and social result of the gift, have produced misery and degradation and immorality from which no one can see the issue; and if the feeling which prompted these gifts is to be called a Christian one, much more truly must that be called Christian which aims at enlightening and directing relief, so that it may reach those to whom it will do real permanent good, the thoughtful and critical spirit which has produced a better administration of the poor law and has established the societies for the organisation of charity.

2. Christian teaching needs emphatically the exercise of this critical spirit. In the exposition of the Scriptures how vast are the advantages which have been gained by the critical handling of the Bible during the last 300 years; how much more complete a source of edification have the sacred books become; how much more real they have become by becoming more human; how much more clearly does the character and work of Christ stand out; how much better is our prospect of dispelling illusions and needless controversies. In Christian teaching all the fuller extension and application of Gospel truth lies in that sphere in which the critical spirit can operate as a regulating power. It is well to preach the elementary truth of the forgiveness of sins; but to guide men with careful judgment into a holy life is better. To fan their hopes of immortality is right; but so also is it right to show them how to live as Christians here. It is a Christian thing to lead men in prayer and praise, and to preach to them; but still more is it a Christian thing to induce them to conse-crate their common life, day by day, to justice and

purity, to steady and unselfish labour. If a sceptical
and desponding temperament sometimes drives us
back from immortal hopes or from the joy of uplifting
prayer, it may serve to make us appreciate more highly
the sanctity of plain duties, to work out the problem
of life by finding the moral equivalents of those high
spiritual feelings to which for the time we cannot attain.

3. As regards the Christian spirit, much of the
religion of our day is tinged with an unreal sentiment
and evaporates in exaggeration ; much is tainted
with clericalism. If we feel these evils strongly, how
can we help longing that they may be purged out by
that which the prophet called " The spirit of judgment
and the spirit of burning." And when the unreality
and the clericalism are exposed and recognised as
evil, if men should feel for a time a certain mistrust of
all high spiritual effort, yet the same sober spirit may
come in and say, " The blessed life is still open before
you, and Christ is still its source and His spirit presides over its destinies. Love must be encouraged,
social good must be pursued ; the backward classes
must be raised, the degraded nations of mankind
must be instructed. Education, temperance, sanitary
welfare, knowledge, art, refinement, political justice,
must be pursued. In these also religion lies ; by
means of these, which are truly Christian efforts, the
world may be won to God."

I entreat those who love Christ not to be alarmed
by the critical questioning spirit that is abroad, but to
look upon it as at least a possible ally of the practical

ministry of the Gospel. Even when it is in the extreme, and when we cannot join with those in whom
it is over-active, we may yet recognise in it a wholesome antidote to the opposite extremes of exaggerated assertions, of hypocrisy and of unreality. But
when it is not thus extreme, and we can find a point
of contact with its possessors, let us welcome it as a
necessary element of the Christian life. Let us submit
ourselves, our views, our plans to its influence. Let us
pray not only that our faith may be increased and our
zeal abound, but that, by the pruning process of criticism, our faith may be sobered and our zeal well directed. So the questioning spirit may help us to do
more good.

The present day is one in which the spirit of per-
secution is dormant, if not dead. No one has the in-
tention of provoking the persecutions for mere opinion
which even in recent times have agitated the Church.
It is not indifference that is the cause of this, but
rather the growing belief that differences, doubts, even
denials are often the expressions of the deepest conviction. The Church, I think, is unwilling to forego the
benefit which it may gain from spirits of a more critical or sceptical tone ; and every one now is at liberty
to submit his thoughts to his fellow-churchmen in
frank exchange and without fear of blame, so long as
they see that this is done with sincerity, in a Christian
spirit, and with a wish to do good. Let us seize on
the happy opportunity, while the dogs of war and controversy are asleep, to draw together those tendencies

which ought to be friends, though they have been so long parted that they are assumed to be natural enemies—the spirit of patient and laborious criticism, and the spirit of patient and laborious pastoral activity.

And I entreat also those who are themselves prone to critical inquiries, and are of a somewhat sceptical temper, not to allow this to draw them away from Christian usefulness and pastoral activity. It is quite certain that among the practical people of England to whom duty and faith are real, the more liberal ideas in theology never can establish themselves unless they are found to result in some distinct moral and religious good. And for this we do not require to invent some new system. The regular parochial system of our Church, which embraces every Englishman who lives within the parochial boundaries, and freely invites him, without any curious inquiry into his special tenets, to act as a Christian, and to join in good works for the benefit of all, lends itself most readily to this combination of a less dogmatic theology with earnest pastoral activity, if only it be administered in a liberal and hearty spirit. But there is in many persons who are of a critical temper a tendency of mind which may be likened to low spirits in the physical organisation, a tendency to give up hope, and with hope to give up effort. You have lost your illusions, you say, and do not expect all the good which many excellent men in their innocence anticipate. No, not all the good; but will you give up the

game, and let all the evil come ? You cannot do all
good, but you may do some; let the sense of frequent
failure not make you despond, but stimulate you to
aim at excellence. You may never attain your ideal;
but to aim at it elevates all your attempts. When you
have learnt that all is vanity, you may still see that
there are many such vanities which are well worth
possessing, nay, which are indispensable, though they
may be temporary. They are shadows, dreams, illusions to those who seek selfish enjoyment in them ;
but they have a reality hid within them for all to
whom truth and virtue are paramount. As you lay
hold on them with the resolution to use them as God
meant them and not otherwise, they will grow more
firm in your grasp, for the very sacrifice and the effort
of seizing them makes them real ; and you will find
that in the discovery of truth, and in the practical
ministry to the wants of your fellow-men, life recovers
the reality of which a too-restless criticism would by
itself have tended to deprive it.

And if not to the critic himself, yet to the Church
and the world at large, the pruning and negative
process may liberate the truth, and intensify the zeal
with which it is preached. Let the thought of a
distant mechanical God disappear ; the immanent
God, the Spirit, will be all the more felt living through
the creation, and through our souls. Let the overweening estimate of the element of public worship disappear ; the sober and chastened worship whose words
are few will be all the more a worship in spirit and in

truth.   We may have a shorter creed to expound, but the simple doctrine of a Divine love which has saved us will stand out, as it has done in all reforming periods, the more brightly.   We may theorise less about the person of Christ ; but the image of His character, the reality of His life and His divine self-sacrifice will grow more intense and vivid.   We may not distract our hearers by the preaching of disputed difficulties, but this will set us the more earnestly upon expounding the life of faith and duty, and applying Christian principle to the whole circle of human affairs.   We may assert less about the future, whether here or hereafter ; but we shall see and take part in the process by which the kingdoms of the world are becoming the kingdom of God and of Christ, and the sounder and soberer assurance will grow in us more and more that the life which is spent for the good of others is in itself divine and immortal, and that, as we have some experience here of a God of love working in us and making us work for others in communion with Him, we and those for whom we labour shall live to Him beyond the grave.

VI.

The Universal Priesthood of Believers.

VI.

The Universal Priesthood of Believers.

(Preached before the University of Oxford, February 19, 1882.)

"An holy priesthood, to offer up spiritual sacrifices."—I PETER ii. 5.

THE Apostle's doctrine of the universal priesthood of believers has been commonly maintained as a negative rather than as a positive assertion. It has been used to controvert the idea that there is in the Church a sacerdotal order. The object of the present sermon will be to set forth the positive meaning of it, and to draw out its practical consequences.

The memorable words in which Bishop Lightfoot opens his essay on the Christian ministry present a good instance of the negative use of the doctrine. Almost every clause of it is a negative in its bearing, if not in form. "The kingdom of Christ," he says, "not being a kingdom of the world, is not limited by the restrictions which fetter other societies, political or religious. It has no sacred days or seasons, no special sanctuaries, because every time and place alike are holy. Above all, it has no sacerdotal system. It interposes no sacrificial tribe or class between God and man, by whose intervention alone

God is reconciled, and man forgiven." He does, however, glance, before dismissing the subject of universal priesthood of believers, at the positive aspect of it. In the original idea of the Church, he says, "every member of the human family was potentially a member of the Church, and, as such, a priest of God. The influence of this idea on the moral and spiritual growth of the individual believer is too plain to require any comment; but its social effects may call for a passing remark. It will hardly be denied, I think, by those who have studied the history of modern civilisation with attention that this conception of the Christian Church has been mainly instrumental in the emancipation of the degraded and oppressed, in the removal of artificial barriers between class and class, and in the diffusion of a general philanthropy, untrammelled by the fetters of party or of race; in short, that to it mainly must be attributed the most important advantages which constitute the superiority of modern societies over ancient. Consciously or unconsciously, the idea of a universal priesthood, of the religious equality of all men, which, though not untaught before, was first embodied in the Church of Christ, has worked, and is working, untold blessings in political institutions, and in social life. But the careful student will also observe that this idea has been very imperfectly apprehended; that, throughout the history of the Church, it has been struggling for recognition, at most times discerned in some of its aspects, but at all times wholly ignored in others; and that, therefore, the actual results are a very inadequate measure of its efficacy, if only it could assume due prominence, and were allowed free scope in action." This idea, which the Bishop says has been "imperfectly apprehended," I wish, with those who hear me, to endeavour to apprehend, and to see what its efficacy would be if it had the due prominence given it of which the Bishop speaks.

A few words must be said as to the application of the word Priest, and of sacrificial language generally, to the life and duties of Christians. The New Testament is the reality, the Old is the shadow. The institutions of the Jewish law were special and limited forms, which were assumed for the time, by great principles, of which the fulness is disclosed in the Christian dispensation. The names which denote these special and transitory forms may be either restricted to these forms themselves, or may be appropriated to the full principles disclosed in the later age. It is certain that to the writers of the New Testament, the word Priest, when not applied to the sacrificial functionaries of the Jews, implied a spiritual function of every believer. It never once is applied by them to the officers of the Christian community. It did not summon up to their minds the ceremonies of public worship, but the acts of common life. And this mode of speech became habitual with the early fathers. These fathers, says Bishop Kaye, used a language directly opposite to that which counts the New Testament use of these words as merely meta-

L

phorical. "They regarded the spiritual sacrifice as the true and proper sacrifice, the external sacrificial act as merely the sign and symbol." In modern times, while the word sacrifice, in its true spiritual sense, has passed into all the languages of Christendom, the word Priest is no longer used as the Apostles and the early fathers used it : and we might be contented to discard the word, and to speak in more common language of serving God, and doing good to men in God's name. But perhaps the high religious sanction which we desire to vindicate for the functions of common life will be best kept before our mind if we use the words Priest and Priesthood ; for we desire to represent the true life distinctly as a life of consecration.

We have to speak first of the recognition of the priesthood of all believers, secondly of the exercise of this priesthood.

I.—The powers involved in the idea of priesthood are to be recognised as present throughout the Christian community. This will appear if we take separately the functions in which priesthood is shown, sacrifice, absolution, and blessing our brethren. To each of these we must give an entirely spiritual sense, and one in which it may at once be seen that every believer can take part.

I cannot doubt that the root idea of sacrifice, that which was struggling for recognition throughout the long development which found its culmination in the sacrifice of Christ, is contained in the words, "Present your bodies a living sacrifice, holy, acceptable to God, which is your reasonable service." This found an outward expression in many forms under the old dispensation. Men gave to God in contrition or in deprecation of evil, or in gratitude, or (as in the whole burnt-offering) as a token of their absolute consecration to Him. But the spiritual idea of sacrifice is brought out again and again, in words such as those of the 51st Psalm, "The sacrifice of God is a broken spirit: a broken and a contrite heart, O God, Thou wilt not despise." In the new dispensation, in conformity with the whole New Testament teaching, the inner principle is unveiled, and is left to work itself out freely in a life consecrated to God. The priesthood of Christ and of His followers combined is expressed in the fullest manner in the words of His high priestly prayer, "For their sakes I sanctify (dedicate, or consecrate, or offer) myself, that they also may be sanctified (dedicated, consecrated, or offered up) through the truth." He who thus consecrates himself is a priest in the only true sense ; and of a life so consecrated every act is a sacrifice. We may follow this up by showing how this principle of self-sacrifice acts in various parts of human life. The renunciation of gain or pleasure for God's sake, the cheerful acceptance of a lower life when we see that the higher is beyond our reach, the readiness to take pains for others, the conscientious discharge of common duties, self-denying rectitude in commerce and society, the unselfish pursuit of scientific truth, frankness, generosity, patriotism, are all forms of the same principle, acts of spiritual sacrifice. Prayer and praise, whether private or public, are also expressions of it, so far, but so far only, as they sum up the sincere outgoing of the heart and life.

The second function of priesthood is absolution; and this must mean to us, a right moral judgment, with the comfort and assurance which this enables us to impart. Can we doubt that in this power every believer shares? If we appeal to the words of our Lord, " Whose sins ye remit, they are remitted unto them," it is certain that these words were spoken not to any class within the little Christian community, but to them all, to all the band, " the number of whose names together were about 120." If we look at the two cardinal instances of the exercise of the power which the New Testament presents, the absolving of the Gentile Christians from the yoke of the law with all the offences incident to it, the absolving of the sinner at Corinth from his excluding guilt, in each case it is all the members of the Church by whom the sentence is pronounced. Or if we reason upon this power, and say that its meaning is to be found not in any formal sentence (since no man can change the facts or make the guilty innocent), but in a spiritual insight which perceives and declares the guilt or the pardon, we see that this is a purely spiritual act, dependent not on hierarchical position but upon spiritual capacity, and, therefore, to be exercised by all according to their actual spiritual power. The sentence or, if we so choose to call it, the sacrament of absolution can be only the imparting of the assurance of forgiveness; and this assurance each believer can impart according to the measure of his faith, his spiritual insight, and his power of sympathy.

The last priestly function is the duty of blessing our brethren in God's name. But blessing must be taken by Christians as applying not to formal words of blessing, but to the conveyance of spiritual peace and happiness. Who will say where these may be obtained? We have gained them, surely, as often from the humblest as from the most learned, from children as from mature Christians, from laymen as from clergymen, from women as from men, in the family as in the place of worship, through letters and printed words as through the voice and presence of those we reverence.

II.—Thus far I have dealt with the first part of the subject, the recognition of the universal priesthood of believers. But it is of far greater importance to point out how this recognition may be made practical, or, to use again the words of Bishop Lightfoot, what would be "its efficiency if only it could assume due prominence and were allowed free scope in action."

1. The overweening importance attached to public worship and to the clerical functions connected with it would be reduced, and that of the other priestly acts of believers would largely increase. There is a tendency of our thoughts, as soon as religion is spoken

of, to fly at once to the scenes of public worship.
And, if we observe a conversation on religious topics,
if not in University circles where men reason more
deeply, yet in ordinary society, in newspapers, and in
political discussion, we almost always find it eventuate
in questions relating to congregational worship. The
hollowness of this tendency has appeared to some
minds of great insight so fatal, that they have wished
or believed that public worship might cease altogether
in the Church. Heinrich Heine said that the one
thing which was detestable among Jews, Protestants,
and Catholics, was public worship. · Even Richard
Rothe, one of the most large-minded and the most
deeply pious of German theologians, declared his conviction that the Church as an organisation for worship
was destined to dwindle and pass away. It is not
necessary to share these gloomy views ; for, however
much we may recognise the work of the Spirit in
other departments than that of public worship, all
who work in those departments need a common
meeting-place and the maintenance of common
aspirations, and a constant renewal of their common
relations to God, and this is specially found in public
worship. Blessed, thrice blessed, on these accounts,
will the assembling of ourselves together ever be to
the great majority of Christians. But where public
worship and its appurtenances take a place which is
hardly less than all-absorbing and exclusive, it is
necessary to point out the bad results which flow
from this usurpation. A great part of the Christian

instruction and energy which ought to flow forth in fortifying the common life of men is absorbed in the details of worship and the attempt at over-minute definitions of religious truth apart from human life. Men are divided from each other on questions about rites, or about the ministers of worship, instead of being united in the great bond of the Christian life. And the clergy, who are the ministers of public worship, come then to be a supreme and exclusive class within the Christian body : so that when men speak of the Church they much more frequently mean the clergy and the system of worship than the re-deemed community and its life. The remedy for this is not so much to be found, as was done to some extent at the Reformation, and as has been done exclusively in the revolutionary movements of this century, in abasing the status of the clergy, but much more in raising up the functions of the laity. It is not the clergy, even according to the celebrated saying of M. Gambetta, but clericalism which is the enemy ; and its antidote is that the whole Christian body should learn to say " We are the Church," and that every man in his vocation should feel that he is exercising a sacred ministry as truly as the man who leads in prayer or speaks from the pulpit.

This view of the Christian Church may rightly be called the primitive view. The ministries of the early Church, as research into its origins has shown us, were formed not for worship but for government. Worship was left free under the shadow of the rule that all should be done decently and in order. The ruling elders were not, as some of the early Presbyterians supposed in the theory combated by Hooker, exceptional officers apart from the rest, but the whole body of the elders, some of whom, as some of every class, took part in the conduct of divine worship. If it is thought by some that some of these conclusions have been overdrawn, still I think no one can doubt that the organisation of the early Churches was framed rather for administering the affairs of the whole community as a society for mutual well-doing than for the conduct of common worship.

The whole community, then, in the whole range of its life to which government and mutual well-doing apply, is, in the Christian sense, a kingdom of priests ; and every act of a faithful life is a sacrifice. And if we carry this principle to its furthest consequences, we cannot doubt that the ideal of the Church which should be kept before our eyes is that of an all-embracing community, endowed with supreme sovereignty, and exercising all its functions in the name and spirit of Christ. It may be wrong to suppose that we can act on this supposition as though this state was already attained. But of this we may be sure, that there will be unrest and distraction in human affairs until the Church is sovereign, that is, until the nation and the state are distinctly pervaded by the Christian principle. The attempts to bring this about which have been made at various epochs, by Savonarola at Florence, by Calvin at Geneva, by those who organised the English state before and at the Reformation on the assumption that it was one great spiritual whole or body politic, and again the attempts of the Puritans to found colonies in America, where they could live their whole life according to the laws of God, have all met with but very partial success. But they have been in the right direction, and it must be the task of our age to press on in that direction and to dedicate the whole life of man to God.

2. But, leaving this great ideal, we may apply our principle to the state of the Church as we find it now. There is the inner circle of Church life, that is, the organisation for worship, instruction, and beneficence, which is conducted under the leadership of the parochial clergy. The object of all who have to do with this should be not to overlay the system with the sole, autocratic, separate priesthood of the clergy, but, on the contrary, to evoke, to the fullest extent, the germs of priestly consecration and sacrifice, the service of the individual members of the parochial Church. We must train them to this service. And, where we see any disposition for this service, we must recognise this with the heartiest readiness, as the spontaneous movement of the Holy Spirit, a sacred thing which we have no right to interfere with. For order's sake, we must, of course, take care that the various activities do not clash with one another; and we must, from time to time, guard men against movements

which are eccentric and are found by experience to be
unprofitable. But to make any system of our own or
any traditional type the measure of God's work, to
insist that all that does not agree with such a system
shall cease or be driven out, what is this but to
thwart and to quench the Spirit of God ? Instead of
trying to live men's lives for them, we must foster
any original power developed in them. We must
gladly see them form institutions for Christian purposes, and be prepared to let such institutions be
moulded according to their conceptions rather than
our own. It is this which gives so real a spiritual
force to the proposals which are made from time to
time to give definite constitutional power to the laity
in parishes. So long as such proposals are looked
upon merely as a drag upon the clergyman, they are
weak. But when they partake of the true character
of Christian constitutionalism, which means the combining of the free spiritual power of each into the
energy of the whole, they have with them the strength
which comes from a consciousness of the divine in-
dwelling. They mean the drawing forth in men's
souls of the powers of counsel and care for their
fellows, the unsealing of fountains of precious waters
of beneficence which have been pent up, the opening
of mines from which the golden store of Christian
service, which has hitherto lain useless, may come
forth to enrich mankind.

3. This suggests another aspect of our subject, the
respect which is due from us to those religious move-

ments and religious communities which have formed
themselves spontaneously amongst us. However
much we may have been vexed at times by extrava-
gance or contentiousness, or dogmatism, or the mere
spirit of dissidence, how infinitely precious is anything
of original Christian conviction! When we sojourn
in France or in Italy, where a servile Church system
has made religion frivolous and reasonable faith all
but impossible; or even in Germany, where officialism
has so cramped it, we are almost impelled to cry out,
" Oh! for one movement of dissent in any of its forms,
of the free conviction with which the Christian Anglo-
Saxon has learnt to take his stand in the presence of
earth and heaven, not bowing down to an authority
he cannot believe in, but obeying his conscience as
supreme." All forms of such honest conviction, from
the Roman Catholic, who bears a lifelong ban
amongst us rather than give up his faith, to the
Theist, who dares not utter more than the first
article of the Creed (nay, have we not said at times, in
our more hopeful moods, to the Agnostic, whose dumb
faith fears to go beyond the truth, even in affirming
the existence of God?), from the sedate worship and
full-formed system of respectable and political non-
conformity to the noisy confusion of the Salvation
Army, have made some real contribution to the
spiritual life of the race, and must be respected and
valued by us as phases, however strange, of the
universal priesthood of believers.

4. We may here touch upon the sense of in-

dividual independence as intimately connected with
the idea of priesthood. The priest is consecrated by
God Himself. No man may interfere with him. It
is a kind of sacrilege which we commit when we
overbear individual conviction, or interfere beyond
the just limits with individual action.   St. Paul
guarded his independence even against the supposed
authority of the most intimate disciples of Christ ;
and in this, as in his call to be a Christian, he is an
example to all believers. Great boldness was the
characteristic of the early Christian teachers ; and it
ought to be so with us.   Will it be said that boldness
has run into excess in our time, and that the wildest
opinions are often maintained ?   I reply, first, that
wild assertions made by those who do not care to
harmonise the various parts of human life are hardly
worthy of notice ; but, secondly, that when we. have
fully framed our views, in humility and with prayer,
the best service and sacrifice that we can render to
God and to man is to speak out our thoughts with
boldness, and to strive with energy to give them
effect. And the best influence we can exert upon
other men is that which will foster in them such
convictions, and win for them the opportunity of
expressing them.   Mere recklessness of assertion
or impulsiveness of action is, indeed, a great danger,
and it is generally swayed by an unconscious
deference to some assumption which has not been
fathomed, but is taken on authority. That is not
true independence. But thorough and original con-

viction, even though its expression is one-sided, is always precious, and its ministry will very rarely be unfruitful. Nor need this be original in the sense of being strange. The most ordinary view of life, if he who entertains it is sincere, is much more fruitful than the most novel idea caught up at second-hand. Let our effort be to realise, to appropriate ; let us act because we feel and are convinced, and because we see that what we are doing can be a channel for the outflow of love. Let us never be ashamed of our thoughts or our actions, nor of connecting them distinctly with our allegiance to Christ. This will be our truest sacrifice, a sacrifice which will not fail of a reconciling effect upon our fellow-men.

5. With this independence we may connect the sense of dignity. As the priestly consecration made the commonest things holy, and rendered them the channels of grace to others, so every work that is undertaken in faith becomes a holy offering and a channel of good. There is nothing which gives a deeper impression of the redemptive power of Christianity than the teaching which St. Paul addressed to slaves. He is not so anxious that they should obtain external freedom, but much more that they should view their service as rendered to God : " With good-will doing service as unto the Lord and not to men." In this way they were to show that, though outwardly bondsmen, they were spiritually independent. Their service became a ministry, a Christian sacrifice. And it is in the same light that we are to view all our

Christian life. Each of the various functions which we fill is a priesthood; the service which we render in them is a holy sacrifice; the materials which we employ are sacraments and signs of the spiritual act within. The student who devotes himself to the acquisition of truth, whose prayer is that his mind may be sustained till he has acquired the knowledge which it is his duty to seek, is ministering in a sacred office, and his writings, up from the simplest college essay or analysis to the highest product of genius, the outward record of the working of his spirit within, are the emblems and signs of his ministry. The trader who is determined to act honestly and is conscious that his trade is the means of benefit to others, and follows it with that object, is a minister of God for their good, and the commodities with which he deals are the outward sign of his honesty and his beneficence. The artist whose object is beauty is, by purifying and ennobling our sense of beauty, doing service to God and man, and the works of his art are the media by which his service is rendered. And if, as we have been assured of late by a high priest of art, we are not to measure works of art by an exclusively moral standard, or to require that they should read a religious lesson, yet the refinement and the repose which they bring are part of our moral nature; and the artist may justly feel that through his works, as through a sacramental channel, priceless blessings may flow to his fellow-men. I need not point out that the same is true in the family where

every father is a priest by a kind of natural consecration, nor in the State where every ruler is a minister of
God for our good. The great want of our age is that
we should look at all these functions not as profane
and secular, according to the heathen and Jewish idea
which Christ came to banish, but as those in which
the service of God pre-eminently lies. There is the
true sacrifice, there the living priesthood, there is the
sacrament of our union, the real presence and the
body of Christ our Lord.

6. In our day, and especially in this University,
this is the aspect of Christianity on which it most
behoves us to dwell. It is an age of much movement
of opinion, and the dogmatic and sacerdotal systems
with which Christianity has been bound up in past
ages have lost much of their hold on mankind.
There is a demand on all sides for a religion which
shall be a life rather than a system. It is true, no
doubt, that all serious life involves principles which
can be stated in a dogmatic form, and also that it
must have some system or polity in which to move.
But what is demanded is that the life should be
paramount, and dogma and system secondary ; that
is, that the free life of the spirit should not be
cramped either by statements or by rules ; that, so
far as statements are made, they should be made
with the recognition that they are attempts to
express a divine life which is beyond all expression,
and that they should be constantly tested by the
living experience of souls in contact with the divine ;

and that Church systems should be sufficiently elastic to give free play to the diverse action of the Spirit which blows where it lists. Under these conditions we may freely use the language and the institutions bequeathed to us by the piety of former ages. But it may well be that these may so change their form as, for a time, to be hardly recognisable, or may even undergo some eclipse. And what all who love Christ should seek to do is to foster the religion of life and duty as distinguished from a religion of acts of worship; for this is the sacrifice which all can offer. And those to whom Church services have grown dim, and sermons dull, may find—let us aid them in finding—in conscientious research, or earnest political discussion, in art, or in family and social intercourse, or in the works of Christian philanthropy, a dogma of the spirit, a ritual of life, through which the holy and acceptable service can be rendered to God.

Education is advancing, and more and more men are becoming able to instruct one another. The press is a great engine which dispenses the pulpit from some part, at least, of its work, and replaces the symbols of Christian worship by the realities of life. The long-drawn ritual of the middle ages, the many hours' preachings and didactic prayers of the Puritan era, found their reason, to a large extent, in the fact that they were the means of popular instruction; they did the work of the school and the press as well as that of public worship. We all acquiesce in the change by which the extra-ecclesiastical life has been enlarged, and the intra-ecclesiastical life has been straitened. How far is this process destined to go on? That we can hardly tell. But we can look at the question with the utmost calmness if only the extra-ecclesiastical life can become Christian and spiritual. On this condition, let the process I have described go on ever so far, it will only mean that the Church itself, the body of believers, is rising to its true position, becoming conscious of itself and of its vocation; that worship is no longer confined to the sanctuary, but spreading itself through the life of mankind; that the limited priesthood of the leaders of public prayer is being exchanged for the universal priesthood of believers.

Lastly, we pray for the progress of the Gospel, and for the evangelisation of the masses in our towns. How can we expect this to be brought about till, by the recognition of the principle I am developing, the latent powers of all believers are drawn out? The great thing to be desired is, that righteousness, and the fear of God, should pervade the community; and this can only be accomplished by the work of individuals helping one another, like the stones supporting each other in the building. We should desire to see centres of Christian influence multiplied on all sides, sound principle and care for the spiritual welfare of men working its way from heart to heart, from life to life. We must teach men and women of all classes that they are not to be mere hearers, nor individual recipients of spiritual good, but sources of spiritual

M

good to those who are connected with them. We must say to them, "It is not the clergy alone to whom the duty of religious influence is committed. You yourselves are responsible for it. Take your part, each as you can, in the works of Christian instruction and beneficence. Let each be a priest in his family, and in his trade or profession, and in the society in which he moves, so that Christ may become the bond of union to every company, the ultimate touchstone and standard of appeal for all consciences, and for every act." It is by this open system of living religion which dwells in the fresh air that we shall summon the breath to breathe from the four winds upon the dead and the indifferent, that they may live. It is certain that the co-operation of all, in all the functions which they fill, is needed to effect the purposes of our ministry. It is by this that the promise may by degrees come to be fulfilled, that all shall know the Lord from the least to the greatest. The coming of Christ's kingdom in its fulness awaits the recognition, and the practical exercise, of the universal priesthood of his servants.

VII.

God Immanent in Man and Nature.

M 2

VII.

God Immanent in Man and Nature.

(Preached at Balliol College, May 21, 1882.)

"God is a Spirit: and they that worship Him must worship Him in spirit and in truth."—JOHN iv. 24.

WHO is there who has not at times been perplexed when he has tried to think of God ? What is God ? Where is He, and how shall we find Him ? When philosophers speak of Him as the Great First Cause, or the Infinite, and the Absolute, such words fall too coldly on our ears and on our hearts to evoke any earnest response. If we try to conceive Him after the likeness of a man, we soon fall into unworthy ideas or run counter to facts. We seize upon the image of goodness presented in the human personality of Christ, and say that "In Him dwelleth all the fulness of the Godhead bodily." But that personality has passed away from the earth, and a merely historical religion becomes impossible to us. We seem to be hemmed in by the difficulty of finding God. Out of that difficulty a way seems to be shown us in the words, "God is a Spirit."

That is the declaration which the Ascension and Whitsuntide make. The form of the Son of Man passes away, and the Spirit comes. We are no longer to think of the Divine as confined within the personality of a man, though that personality represents with the utmost vividness God in history. It was expedient that that should pass away, and that which was better, which was to come instead, was the Spirit, the essential and final manifestation of God to man—that which is the inner fountain of the Divine life, that by which God makes Himself known, not to the outer sense, but to the inner conviction and the heart of man. This declaration is peculiarly appropriate to our own time, when much doubt is thrown upon the external mechanism of religion, whether in its ancient documents or its present forms, but when the spirit of religion is very far from being denied, nay, is often felt and accepted far beyond the limits of churches and confessions of faith. May we not find that a God who is felt, and who becomes a living power to us, though we can hardly express in a logical statement what that power is, is more real to us than a God fenced in all round by guarantees and attested by historical documents ?

For what is meant by saying that God is a Spirit ? First, God is an influence, a power which we feel working upon us and upon the world generally—as it has been said by a great writer of our day, " A stream of tendency," "A power that makes for righteousness." But it would be wrong to insist upon such an expression as this as adequate ; for the comparison is somewhat dangerous which likens the chief power in the

world to a material and unconscious thing—a stream.
Whatever the supreme power is, He cannot be thought
of as destitute of mind and love. If we cannot take
the human mind and human love as wholly realising
the true conception of Him, it is because we must
conceive of Him as infinitely transcending these. He
cannot be less than our thought or our love, but infinitely more ; embracing these, but embracing a vast
circle of energy beyond them. We speak of man as
being essentially a spiritual being, and St. Paul leads
us to argue from the spirit of a man, which knows the
things of a man, to the Spirit of God, which knows the
things of God. But, just as we may think of a man as
the centre of influences which emanate from him, as
breathing forth upon the whole circle of his family
and friends an atmosphere of kindness, or refinement,
or knowledge, of which they all come to partake—just
as we speak of the spirit of a man's life, and the spirit
which he sheds around him, so we may think of God
as the centre of all the Divine influence which quickens
and sustains, which comforts and encourages us,
which brightens the mind and gives fervour to the
moral affections, which combines all the forces of the
world so as not only to make but to work for
righteousness. The world is the vesture of the
unseen God ; its whole atmosphere is charged with
His presence. Whosoever, in humble faith, and with
a heart which longs for truth and goodness, opens his
mouth and draws in his breath, that man is straight-
way filled, not with some vague influence only, but

with all the fulness of God. The desire and the power to do right which he acquires is none other than the central force which animates the world. He lives and moves in God.

The tendency of modern thought is to trace a single power working throughout the universe; to presume that it is one force, constant, yet changing its mode of action, by which man and nature alike are swayed. Does not this suggest to us the mode of life of the Divine Being, and of His relation to the world? Is it not quite of a piece with that which is meant by saying that God is a Spirit—that is, an inner power, an influence, a life which penetrates all things, and forms them at its will? It gives us the idea of a God who is not far off, not working merely from without upon His creatures, but within them, the life of their life, the love of their love. The writers on Christian evidences have often likened the action of God upon the world to the action of a mechanic or an architect on the material out of which he makes a watch, or a steam-engine, or a building. But this comparison fails in this point, that there is no evidence of any such agent working upon the world from without. Perhaps we may gain a more living conception of God by speaking of Him as the soul of the world, and comparing His action to that of the vital power in man upon his body; or, in animated nature, to the action of the inner principle of life upon the particles of matter which make up the organism. That last is a constructive and an upholding energy, and gives us a truer view of creation than the other.

Further, this thought of a Divine Spirit working through us and through all things gives us a sense of unity, and shows us how the discords without and within us may be harmonised and all be brought under the dominion of God. The love which we feel to be our own true life is no longer thought of as a peculiar endowment of ourselves, or of a few like ourselves. It combines with the larger love, which is the true life of the great family of man, and which centres in Jesus Christ. And this love, again, which is the true life of mankind, has its source in the eternal impulse of life which moves the whole universe; and thus we gain the assurance that that impulse also is one of boundless love. The Word, which was made flesh in Jesus of Nazareth, is He without Whom nothing was made; and that Word is God. Instead of conceiving of the world as a series of separate creations, and miracles, and interpositions, we may conceive of it as a growth, or development, of which God Himself forms the living and directing force.

What we are concerned with in preaching is the effect of this belief in the Divine Spirit upon our lives and consciences. In tracing this out, I will make use of two words, both of them familiar to us, in which we seem to realise the idea of a higher power, of a Holy Spirit, combining with and giving energy to our own —inspiration and aspiration.

1. We have been so much accustomed to think of

inspiration as specially belonging to the writers of the Bible that we fail to realise it as belonging to ourselves. Yet St. Paul's teaching was that every Christian was inspired; and in our familiar prayers and collects we ask for that inspiration which makes us do what is good, and may cleanse the thoughts of our hearts. It is the consciousness that this inspiration is working within us which gives us spiritual power. The Christian doctrine is that the Spirit allies Himself with every faculty of ours to quicken and to strengthen it, and to work through it for good. Who can refuse, without being false to himself, to listen to the conscience by which he perceives right and wrong, and is impelled to choose the one and avoid the other? Why is it, then, that conscience is so often stripped of its due authority, that it grows languid, and even perverted? Is it not because we do not habitually recognise it as the chosen organ of God within us? If we accustomed ourselves to feel that the voice which speaks to us there is His voice and that the impulse towards good is His impulse, and the faculty by which we discern good from evil is the eye of God, must not the light by which we see the truth grow constantly clearer, and the sacred voice sound louder and louder, until its dictates, or rather its drawings, would prove irresistible? We imagine that, if the heavens could open, or the ground cleave asunder, and a voice like the trumpet of Mount Sinai could proclaim the moral law in our hearing, we should at once and for ever be scared from evil and impelled towards good. But the true teaching bids us recognise God in none of these so much as in the still small voice persuading us, reasoning with us, saying, " This is the way, walk ye into it," drawing out to our view the beauty of goodness, humbling us because of our faults, leading us to the fountain of repentance and forgiveness, constraining us by the power of love, bidding us go forth, not with conviction only but with gladness, to do right. And that voice we hear every moment, if we will but listen to it. Let us acknowledge it as supreme, as the voice of God within us.

We need not dwell on the objection that conscience is often weak, sometimes perverted, and that we cannot, therefore, trust it absolutely as the voice of God. I do not think that any one acting with a sincere wish to know truth and right, has ever gone far wrong. We may easily be deceived if our conscience only reflects our habitual standard of duty, and we are closing our minds against fresh light and truth. But the Divine inspiration of which we are speaking may be tested, in distinction from self-deception, by this—that it makes the conscience not blind and fanatical but open-minded and progressive. The Spirit is the spirit of truth, and guides those into whom it enters into all truth.

The voice of the Spirit is spontaneous, immediate. It may, indeed, make use of many means, but none of them is absolutely essential. It may speak to us through historical scenes, or through the words of

Christ or the Apostles, or through the prayers and sacraments of the Church, or through sermons ; or it may make use of things passing before our eyes, of events in public or private life ; or, again, of thoughts suggested by study or by conversation. Through all these it may bring about conviction. But, by whatever means the truth may be, impressed upon us, it is the Divine Spirit which speaks through them ; and when we are in contact with the truth itself, the medium is of little importance. The influence of the Spirit is like the electric current, which may pass through many intricate coils, but conveys its force and flashes its bright light with almost equal rapidity whether the conducting medium be of the smallest or the greatest length. It is not confined to any special mode of operation, nor to any system, nor to any class of men. It works upon all, though in different ways and degrees ; and we can appeal with confidence to the consciousness which all men have of its quickening power, of the light which lighteth every man.

It is not only as an enlightener of the conscience that the Divine Spirit comes to us. His influence is equally felt in our feelings and our actions. He quickens all our powers. ·When once we are convinced, and drawn towards holiness, our faculties are all alive and sustained. The genial warmth makes the life-blood circulate throughout our spiritual frame. We gain quick affections, which fasten upon the good and the noble everywhere. We have power to deny ourselves, because our better self has been aroused, and we come to feel a keener delight in goodness and truth than in selfish pleasure. And we are sustained in a persevering effort to reach the goal of our spiritual desires. The Divine power urges us across mountains and morasses, for we see beyond them the light of our home.

This inspiration is also a social power. In the general, it is true to say that the moral instincts of mankind are right, and the people's voice is the voice of God. The Church in all its branches and organisations is Divine. But we must not stop here. The bonds of secular society are also Divine. Friendship and love and marriage, family ties and those of country, association in art and knowledge, the organisation which exists for civil and political objects, the school, the college, the city, the nation, have all a Divine foundation ; for their object is that which is most Divine, that union of spiritual beings which constantly rises into love ; and love, says St. John, is of God, for God is love. We may trace inspiration yet more widely ; for human nature and the material world can no longer be separated, and the Divine Spirit and purpose can be seen in the harmony which is made by their union. Nor need we fear that we are thus tending to Pantheism, if we keep firmly grasped the fact that the whole is one great unity, and that the moral purpose is its essence, its formal and final cause. There is nothing strange in our having affinity with the brutes and the herbs, with the rocks and the waves, if we acknowledge one Spirit which works through the whole creation till it culminates in human morality and the cross of Jesus Christ. The perception of this is one of the highest effects of inspiration. It is nothing less than the Divine thought inwrought in our minds, the Divine order established in our renewed nature, the surest witness that we are made in the image of God, the spiritual mind by which we see each part of the universe in its relation to its centre, and evolving itself under the Divine purpose towards complete organisation and perfect harmony.

2. This perception, and the consciousness that our nature is the special organ of the Divine Spirit, begets in us a constant *aspiration*. Perhaps it would not be an untrue statement of the doctrine of justification by faith to say that we are saved by aspiration. It is the special property of genuine Christianity not to be contented with the knowledge or goodness which we have attained. The ideal truth, the ideal goodness, lies ever beyond. If we take the character of our Lord, to which alone as Christians we can be pledged, we find there just enough to stimulate the longing for holiness—not a law, not a dogma, not a rule, but a Spirit : not detail enough to make a model which we can copy, nor in the strict sense an example which we can imitate, but an expression of the Divine longing which uplifts and redeems mankind, and which restores the broken harmony of the world. By whatever means this

Spirit enters into us, it exerts an influence over all our nature, which may rightly be called redemptive. We learn to seek those things which are above. We can perceive and express the best, the worthiest side of things. Our own characters are ennobled by the thought of what we may become; our peculiarities become serious bents towards special forms of goodness; our bodily and mental powers are transfigured into spiritual endowments; our common pursuits become part of the process by which we are trained for the higher life beyond us; our studies, part of the culture by which a worthier state is attained; the tests and rivalries to which we are subjected, not in education only, but all through life, become the means of gauging our progress. And as we go on we learn to take part in the redeeming process for other men. We feel that it is not for ourselves alone that we live and aspire, but by our sympathy we carry others with us. For this, perhaps, is the highest form of influence, not one man doing good to another, but one holding the hand of his brother, as saying, "Let us aspire together, God helping us, towards that which is just and pure and true."

A second inseparable effect of this aspiration is spiritual freedom. There can be no constraint where there is conviction and fearless love of truth and longing for goodness. So long as we are uncertain which way to go, we walk in fetters, we hesitate, we take a step and retrace it. You may observe this in speech. Even a great orator halts when he is not

clear as to his purpose. When you read aloud, if
you have not caught the drift of the writer, you read
slowly and doubtfully. But when the purpose is
clear, even a dull man becomes eloquent. So it is
with life generally. If your conscience is clear and
your resolution firm, you can think freely and act
boldly. And he that trusts that this world is all of a
piece, moving with one central impulse of which his
own spirit partakes, feels that he is embarked on the
central current, and that, whatever difficulties he en-
counters, they are but as the rocks which deflect the
stream, or, at most, but minor backwaters for which
he can make allowance. He can be calm, because he
is fearless ; and tolerant, because he knows that all
things make ultimately in the direction in which his
face is set ; and patient, for God waits long, and time
is generally one of the conditions of spiritual success.

A third effect of this aspiration is constant progress. If we know the direction in which we are
going, and are free from the constraint which waits
on uncertainty, we bend all our energies to reach the
goal. That goal for ourselves is holiness and the
image of Christ ; and the stages on the way to that
goal come to view one by one as intermediate objects
of our pursuit. We make progress, we may humbly
hope, in knowledge and in power as our faculties
become stronger ; and we make progress in experience and in opportunities of doing good as life
wears on. We can appreciate also the general progress of mankind, and associate ourselves with it; and

we may thus escape that melancholy condition into which some of the greatest minds seem especially liable to fall, which takes no pleasure in the increasing mastery of man over nature by knowledge and inventions and colonisation. We can feel a genuine thrill at the emancipation of those who are downtrodden, and the advance of education among the masses, and the increase of wealth which enables the poor to gain something of refinement. We can see that in political progress there is involved a spiritual progress, the progress in the realisation of human brotherhood. We can feel also that all true progress is one, and that we advance in union with the whole race of mankind under the impulse and direction of the Spirit of God.

Let us apply this, lastly, to worship. Aspiration is the soul of worship, which is a constant rising towards the object of our adoration. Our Lord said, " They that worship the Father must worship Him in spirit and in truth." St. Paul said, " We are the true circumcision who worship God in the. spirit." The true worship is not the prostration of the body in kneeling, nor even the prostration of the soul in distant adoration, but the yielding of our living powers willingly and gladly to the Divine influence within us. There is an expression of the great stoical emperor, Marcus Aurelius, who perhaps came nearer than any other non-Christian of the West to the Christian life and spirit : " I reverence the God who is within." That God has been fully made known to us in Jesus

N

Christ, and we can give a grander significance to this expression. Our God is within us. Let us allow our thoughts to be enlightened and our energies quickened by the spirit of holiness—the unseen, constraining power of righteousness—and we are practising the true worship. As to the outward form, though it is by no means unimportant, it is of far less account. We must not consider that religion consists in church-going, but must make a great effort to raise the whole life to the dignity of worship, inspiring every part of it with the aspiration towards God. There are some who make much of religious services, and almost seem to identify religion with them; there are others who think religious services have been overdone, and who go so far as to tell us that there are those who have begun to be real Christians from the time when they left off attending Church. There are those who have come from the universities to do Christian work in town who have said that they felt as if in the former no one had ever believed, and in the latter no one had ever doubted, dwelling, no doubt, with exaggerated weight on the fact that a certain number of students here have thrown off the habits of public worship in which they were brought up, and that the upper and middle classes in London mostly attend the Churches. There are those to whom the ordinary services are the very nourishment of their spirits; and there are those who have felt, like our two great Christian poets, Milton and Cowper, neither of whom in their later days attended public worship, that the outward form was a hindrance to their communion with God. We have again to say, "Neither in Jerusalem nor in Gerizim, neither in circumcision nor in uncircumcision ;" or, rather, whether by church-going or by not going to church, through old forms or new—with much ritual or with little, or with none—let the true God, who is a Spirit, be worshipped. Make your choice of means (for some means there must be), not by caprice, nor in carelessness, nor in the desperate plunge of a fretful independence or of a sullen despair, but according to truth and reason, the dictates of conscience, and the drawings of sympathy. Be sincere; let your heart be open to God at all times ; let your service be that of the conscience and the life ; and your eating and drinking, your rising up and lying down, your work and your recreation, your studies, your whole life, will be a communion with God the Spirit, a sacrifice, a prayer, an unceasing worship in spirit and in truth.

VIII.

Intellectual Pursuits and the Higher Life.

VIII.

Intellectual Pursuits and the Higher Life.

(Preached at Balliol College, Oxford, November 24, 1872.)

"And this is the record, that God hath given to us eternal life, and this life is in His Son."—1 JOHN v. 11.

THE eternal life of which St. John speaks is a Divine power, a quickening spirit, which is the spring of all true human life. It is the point at which the life of man comes in contact with the life of God, who is truth and love. This power, having once gained its adequate expression in the life of our Lord, now presents itself to all mankind, seeking to actuate each human soul as it actuated our Lord Himself; and becomes in all who do not through insincerity deny it the constant stimulus to all that is true in thought— to all that is good in act. It is the office of the Christian preacher constantly to apply this stimulus, that the Divine life which was manifested in Christ may be transferred into the lives of those with whom he deals.

I am addressing a company of students, and the studies which find most favour in Oxford are those which are specially called the Literæ Humaniores, or, as the Scotch term them, the "Humanities." Human language, the forms of human thought, the philosophy of human relations or morality, the progress of these

relations worked out in history and fixed by jurispru-
dence, and theology, which views men in their relation
to God—it is to study these mainly that you are here.
And if I take in the social life of a college, which
forms one of its chief advantages, this is but the
practical side of that which in its larger developments
you are studying. This union of life with thought is
what gives such a charm to the studies of this
University. But it also brings with it a great responsibility, for it makes these studies infinitely serious, as
bearing directly on our principles and conduct. As
you decide in such studies as these, so you must pray,
and so you must live when you go out into the world.
There is a habit of mind which takes pleasure in the
mere discussion of views about life apart from any
solid conviction, and against this it is necessary to
guard ; for it is a very dangerous thing to speculate
lightly upon matters of human interest. Our whole
being must go whither our thoughts have led. To a
mind once awakened to the greatness of the issues
involved in the forty or fifty years that lie between
boyhood and death, every fact that bears on his own
destiny and that of his fellows becomes serious.

This seriousness results directly from the consciousness which is aroused by the Spirit of Christ—
the consciousness of God and of immortality. The
eternal life is one in which God is ever present to the
conscience, and it is one which does not end when we
die. This consciousness is profoundly *moral*, and the
parent of morality. God is not mere force, nor is

eternity mere endlessness; but God is a father who loves us, and who is training us by constant discipline, a power of good with whom we are called to co-operate. And the immortality which Christ has brought to light is not a negative state of rest, but a scene of active service—the exercise of our whole nature in a sphere into which sin can never enter.

This eternal life it is, the life which is conscious of God and of immortality, which has been lived on earth by Jesus of Nazareth. And His life is not to be looked on as merely a wonderful exception, but as a witness that this eternal life is the heritage of all mankind. It is the light that lightens every man—the life which has been manifested, which has been declared to us, that we may have fellowship with it. It is God sending His Son in the likeness of sinful flesh, and for sin, and thereby condemning sin in the flesh—that is, it shows us that our selfishness is not ineradicable. We are meant for love, not for self-pleasing; and we have a hope not bounded by earthly interests, "A new heaven and earth, wherein dwelleth righteousness." It is no dream of a saint which speaks of believers as incorporated into Christ. That which was the source of His life, the consciousness of God and eternity which made Him to be wholly devoted to truth and to love, becomes also most really in us the source of an imperishable longing for the truth and love which are in Him.

It may be impossible for us to define with any exactness this eternal life. Like physical life, or love, or righteousness, it is beyond our definitions. And those who lay stress upon the Christian *life* rather than upon any special system may expect, but must calmly accept, a charge of vagueness. The vagueness is that of the subject itself; and it is not in this place that we ought to need to be reminded that definitions are to be exacted only according to tle subject matter. The great things of the human spirit and of God are even less than those of moral science susceptible of the exact definitions which men have unreasonably sought for. But this does not make the Christian life less convinced or less resolute. It may not feel able to pronounce upon questions belonging rather to the domain of metaphysics or of historical inquiry than to what is truly spiritual. But it will not say less confidently that God is light and God is love, and that nothing mean or false or unkind can possibly proceed from Him, or be tolerated by His children. Here is the true field for the positiveness and the vehemence of the Christian Spirit.

But, again, this positiveness, which subordinates all our being to the paramount demands of truth and love, is no narrow feeling exalting one part of human nature to the disparagement of the rest. It recognises human nature as an organic whole, and puts the head where the head should be. But it has sympathy with all that is genuine and good, wherever it may be displayed. It recognises the germ and the yearning where there is but inadequate fulfilment. It can believe that Christ's Spirit has been at

work where Christ's name has not been known. It
is always sure that truth and goodness are of God
wherever they may be found, and that true faith is no
fettering thing, but the liberator of the spirit of man
into the region of its fuller and most fruitful development. If at times Christianity has appeared as a
one-sided cultivation of parts of human nature, and
has fostered a self-sacrifice which cared little for truth,
or a sense of brotherhood which was not universal,
this is because its adherents have belied their own
principles. But it cannot be doubted that the eternal
life—the consciousness of God and of immortality—
is the true support and stimulus of all human excellence, not only in the sphere of what is technically
termed religion, but in the realms of thought and of
beauty. Even Schiller, who wished to restore the
graces and the gods of Greece, felt that their loss was
compensated to the poet by the nobleness of chivalry,
and that the deep thought and seriousness of Christianity had been fruitful of the highest graces of the
Spirit. The ancient civilisation, no doubt, possessed
great treasures of science and of art ; but it was from
want of the spiritual conviction which Christianity
supplies that in the decadence of that civilisation
knowledge became rhetorical, sceptical, sectarian, and
superficial, and art frivolous and servile. It is not
Christian teachers only but positive philosophers who
have shown that it was from the lack of a spiritual
bond that the majestic framework of Roman power
became a dull and oppressive mechanism instead of

a living and life-giving organism. The simple brotherhood of the catacombs, not those who reared the palaces of Diocletian, had the secret of the knowledge and art of the future, as well as of its political and social life, in their hands. It is our part, as Christians, under the impulse of the Divine life, to blend into one the great heritage of the past, and to use the appliances of the present day for the enlightenment and elevation of our brethren, whatever be the sphere to which it pleases God to call us. We have not to make the vain attempt to copy the past in any of its phases, not even in the life of our Lord ; for such an attempt is as vain as that other attempt which is sometimes made in our day to ignore all serious religion in the pursuit of physical science or of artistic culture. But we have to bring the Spirit of Christ as a stimulus to bear upon the acquisitions of knowledge and the conduct of life, as directing and restraining, indeed, but still more as stimulating, in all the regions in which our spirits can move.

Let me endeavour to point out, aided by my own recollections, how college life may aid in this great effort.

1. Let our studies themselves be connected, as they readily may be, with that higher morality which is religion. It has been said that all that any university can teach us is the same which our earliest instruction imparted—to read and to write—the faculty, that is, of acquiring and reproducing knowledge. But, while we may admit that the chief result to be expected in our training is the perfecting of the

instrument by which knowledge is gained and passed on to others, this can only be effectually done by exercise in the subjects of knowledge. And, in the great press of practical work in later life, many a man looks back to college days as those in which he gained the rudiments of knowledge on subjects which he has afterwards been quite unable to follow out, but which he still aspires to and greets from afar. And where detailed information cannot be acquired, yet some insight into the general principles cannot fail to be obtained by study. But it is just these general principles which come closest to the centre of humanity, and which, therefore, can most easily be brought in contact with the Divine life, which is its basis. For instance, in the study of moral philosophy and of ancient history, how can any man whose heart has been aroused by the Spirit of God, as shown forth in Christ, fail to ask himself continually this question —How do the teachings of Plato or Aristotle, or of Kant, or of Mill harmonise with the teachings of Christ and His Apostles? How can I trace out the partial disclosures of God's nature and will towards mankind in other histories so as to see more clearly and to estimate aright the light of life which shines in Jesus Christ? It is inquiry such as this, which is intensely practical, that gives a keener relish to study than all the honours which are its more vulgar incentives.

This leads me to another remark. The whole of human knowledge hangs together, and its centre is in humanity itself, and the centre of humanity

is Christian love.   Therefore, let all knowledge, even
to the utmost detail, group itself round the acknowledged centre.   Seize upon each piece of knowledge
that comes to you, and attach it to your own life·
Every fact has something Divine in it.   It comes
in God's order, and may be brought to bear in some
way on your knowledge of men and your own work
among them.   It is easy to see this in history and
in literature, for that alone is literary which has in
some way to do with human nature.   But even in the
pursuit of physical science, it is evident that those
branches which excite the liveliest interest are those
which bear upon the origin and destinies of men, and
that the rest grow in importance the nearer they approach to contact with human life.   Could any one
devote himself to chemistry if there were no such thing
as organic chemistry ?   Or could any one give his life
to geology and physical geography if the earth were
not the habitation of men ?   We want more students
in England who, like those of Germany, will make
research the object of their lives ; but the hope of
our producing them lies in the recognition by practical
men and by students themselves of this high utili-
tarianism which sees the connexion and harmony of the
world, and invigorates the most abstruse studies by the
sustaining interest of their bearing upon human life.

2. Let the work of your future career impart a
steadiness to your work at college.   It may be that
it is not possible to gain at the University much
of the knowledge which will be of use in professional

life. I incline to think that those educated here have too great a contempt for what are called scraps and smatterings of knowledge. Yet it must be admitted that this is not the place for technical and professional training. If we have gained the habit of deeper thought, of going to the root of things, of doing thoroughly what we do, it is best. But this is aided, not marred, by looking on beyond college days, and fixing our aim there. It is aided by an early choice of a profession, which gives a reality and a meaning to all that is being done here. There are distractions, it is true, in the world of business; but there are also dangers of dreaminess in a student's life. I remember one, who had entered with zest into the Oxford studies, and whose danger appeared to be a diffusion of interests and an unpractical philanthropy, being turned to a life of earnest effort in God's service by observing how men of business concentrated their energies on a single point, and how in the advertisements which were meant to impress the minds of the people two or three words alone were repeated again and again. There are many similar ways in which keeping our minds fixed on the real work of life may serve as a corrective or as a stimulant to the work of a student.

3. But this practical work and its preparation here must be viewed in its highest aspect. We must endeavour to purge it from selfish aims, that it may be in union with the eternal life of God, and for this the society of a college and university affords

peculiar opportunities.   Here the sordid interests and
distinctions of wealth or rank are to a great extent
held in abeyance by the higher interests of learning,
and the freshness of youth suggests hopes which
readily ally themselves with the noblest aims.   The
intercourse which a college fosters is the freest, the
friendships which it begets the most intimate, that
can exist between men.   And when young men
exchange their ideas on politics or business or
religion, if they are sometimes wild or impracticable,
they are rarely tainted by the ignoble thought of
worldly success.   It is a golden time that you are
traversing.   The mere pleasure of it may tempt you
to dissipate it in folly ; and the corruption of the best
may become the worst.   Be better advised, and let
its happy moments excite you to the joy of unselfish
thought and action which you may never afterwards
lose.   Is it too much to hope that, where so much
expansion of mind and heart is possible, the highest
matters of religious interest may not be left so much
in the background, where they become unreal and
generate misunderstanding, and that those who
unite so freely in talking of books that interest them,
and share so readily the aspirations they engender,
may at times join in the devotional study of the
Scriptures, and may value the opportunities of
common prayer, whether in public or in private ?
These are surely among the highest incentives and
supports of a noble aim.

They are also among the best preservatives of

purity. With college days there are mixed up in very many cases the associations of reckless folly and evil communications ; and men often fail through fancying that almost every one of their companions is yielding, or else through a kind of pride or disdain which forgets how closely every thing that is best in human nature is associated with purity. Let us recal ourselves constantly to the thought that we belong to Christ. Let us look on into life as a life for God, as a life of duty, and the thought of this will elevate us beyond the temptations which idleness and frivolity inevitably bring. We may hope that our students may deserve increasingly the praise which even now a great French writer gives them, who observes how much less a hold impurity and moral scepticism have upon the English Universities than on those of his own country.

One other point I will urge, in which the associations of the University may greatly conduce to a true Christian life : I mean the charitable judgment which they induce in religious matters. Men come here often from homes or schools in which a particular kind of religion has been taught. But they come, for the most part, with open minds. They soon learn, through the close intercourse of this place, that men of the most opposite views from those in which they have been brought up are yet serious and religious men. This is a most valuable experience, and no amount of disagreement or controversy ought to make us forget it. With some, no doubt, it may

O

issue in a mere change of front, or in passing over
from one polemical camp to another ; but, for the
most part, I trust it issues in a chastening of the
judgment, in a more modest estimate of our own
advantages and a higher one of the advantages we
have yet to gain, in a willingness to honour real
goodness wherever it may be found. If, in addition,
it can help us in presenting to our minds a truer
image of Christ, and incite us to a burning love of
the truth and justice and kindness which were in
Him, while teaching us to see through the peculiar
tenets about which the parties are wrangling, it will
have yielded us the best of the fruits of righteousness.

God has given us eternal life, and this life is in
His Son. Let us accustom ourselves to think of the
life of God as taking shape and body by contact with
the actual life of men ; and let our prayer be that,
through communion with God and with Christ, we
may have the eternal life dwelling in us, and may
show to the world that the Christian spirit is neither
that of eager contention for what is unreal or disputable, nor a contemptuous intellectualism, but humble
truthfulness and love, patiently wrought out in a
reverent and dutiful life.

IX.

"Progress."

O 2

IX.

"Progress."

(Preached before the University of Oxford, Whit-Sunday, 1871.)

"Nevertheless I tell you the truth; it is expedient for you that I go away: for if I go not away, the Comforter will not come unto you; but if I depart, I will send Him unto you."—JOHN xvi. 7.

THESE words, which are so closely connected with the great event of Whitsuntide, form the ground on which we may claim a right to speak of the Christian religion as emphatically the religion of progress. They describe a progress from a state of tutelage to a state of maturity—a progress which at the moment was painful, but which was really beneficial for the believers in our Lord. That had been a blissful state which they had before enjoyed, when they had their Lord present with them, and were guided by His voice and eye; and the disciples naturally desired, like Peter at the Transfiguration, to build a tabernacle for themselves where they were. But they had to learn that that was not the best state for them. It was to be broken up in a moment, and they were to pass on to a better state beyond, in which Christ would be with them, not in outward presence, but through the Spirit.

This is not an isolated fact, but a great principle of the spiritual life. It is better to be led by an inward influence than by any external rule or system. It is better to have those feelings within us which will prompt us to right thought or action than to be told what to think or to do by any, even the wisest and most divine. And this substitution of the inward for the outward guidance is a process which constantly goes on, as God reveals Himself by the Spirit more and more. It is a principle which finds continually new applications, fresh springing developments. For, though at the day of Pentecost the believers gained a · glimpse into the Kingdom of Heaven, and were possessed by the powers of the world to come, yet the Church has had to live out its life amidst worldly influences, and is ever reaching on by stumbling steps, groping in the twilight, towards that Kingdom which was then opened out to its view. As a man who looks across a valley sees the mountain tops on the other side as though they were very near, and yet afterwards has to win his way thither through the darkness of the valley, in which he often loses sight of the object towards which he is advancing, so it has been with development of the Church's life in its progress through time. We are nearer to the full salvation, even if we fail to perceive it as vividly as the Apostles did. But the object which kindled in them such high hopes must kindle them also in us. We are making progress towards that object. We are appropriating more fully the Divine life, and possessing more completely the spiritual blessings for which the first believers hoped. At each stage of our progress the thought is suggested to us again, "Let us rest where we are, let us make ourselves a rule of the past or the present state; for it has been at least fairly good, and we cannot expect to be better than our fathers." Then comes the truer voice, which says, "No! Onward lies the path. In progress alone is blessedness to be found. It is expedient for you that the present condition of things, the discipline which has trained you, the circumstances that are familiar to you, the customs into which you have grown, the persons even whom you have trusted, should pass away; for so alone can your spiritual powers be fully called forth, and the Kingdom of God be within you."

Let us define to ourselves what we mean by progress; for the word, it must be allowed, often suggests vague, and sometimes unchristian and merely negative, ideas. We must set before us as plainly as we can the goal towards which we hope to advance. I understand, then, that the end to which God designs us to attain is the full possession and exercise of our true relations both towards God and towards one another. This implies, in the individual, a development of every power which connects him with God or men, the growth (in the language of Scripture) "into the measure of the stature of the fulness of Christ." It implies, in the larger sphere of God's purposes, a harmony of all souls and of all created things, each fulfilling its own function under the inspiration of Supreme Love—a state which is described in the words of St. Paul, " That in the dispensation of the fulness of time He might gather together in one all things in Christ, both which are in heaven and which are in earth." This object, though developed fully by St. Paul in the Epistles to the Ephesians and the Colossians, yet is found in germ in the earlier teaching. It is implied in the words of our Lord Himself at the Ascension : " All power is given Me in heaven and in earth." It is implied in the preaching of the Apostles at Pentecost, when they proclaim that Christ is exalted to the supreme place in the universe. It is implied in the whole teaching as to the Logos in St. John, which certainly is not only a formative or efficient principle, but also a final cause, an object towards which the whole creation tends. He in whom the world is made is also its destined Lord.

Is the conception thus put before us as our final goal one which can be made the practical object of the efforts of finite beings ? or is it too vast for our realisation ? Vast it is, stupendous ; but not therefore vague. The true reason, God's organ within us, can conceive it and work it out. Doubtless it involves a resolute entering into the Divine purposes, a placing of ourselves, so to speak, at God's standing-point. But we have the right and the power to do this, for we are called the friends of God. The revelation is given us that we may make it our own and shape our course with a view to it. It is vast, it is all-embracing; but none the less it is clear to our spirits, and they know no other rest-ing-place. We are mariners at sea in the evening, but the coast before us bears on it the great and brilliant city which is our bourne; and if it be necessary to keep our eye fixed on the lighthouse in the centre, none the less the heart takes in the whole scene, with its loved companies and its noble build-ings, and with all that is included in the dear names of country and of home.

It is the Kingdom of Christ which is our goal; and we can aim at no smaller object. Fixing our eyes on this, we direct, yet we overpass, the desires for personal forgiveness, for individual sanctification, the bounds of sect and party, the limitations of our country and our age. Looking at this, we surmount the barriers which separate one Church from another, the spiritual from the secular spheres, the history of the Church from that of mankind, the sphere of mental and physical knowledge. The great goal to which we look is the goal of them all; their limita-tions are but of the moment; their harmony is assured in the Kingdom of Christ and of the Spirit.

But while the goal is thus all-embracing, it is the moral and spiritual principle which is the centre; it is love which is the germinal spot from which all the rest is developed. The Kingdom of God spreads out on all sides; but its capital, its central principle, is found in these words of St. Paul: "The Kingdom of God is righteousness, and peace, and joy in the Holy Ghost."

When we define, as the goal of our practical efforts, the attainment and exercise of true moral relations, we must not fritter away our conception by dwelling on those relations separately, nor yet as a mere inorganic aggregate, but distinguish carefully, as the living centre of them, the great spiritual affections—towards God repentance and trust, towards men justice and beneficence; and these combined in the one word love. All the relations of man, whether towards God or towards his fellows, are but expressions of love; all our true efforts on earth are the striving after those relations which love brings about between spiritual beings. And, moreover, all these separate relations are subject to change, while love itself remains. It is true that love cannot subsist as an abstraction; he must gain a home in the unfolding of the several relations of humanity; but this home he builds for himself. The relations and institutions of the Christian life are begotten by love, not love by them. They change from age to age, but love survives. Suspend their operation for a time; nay, sweep them away, if you can; yet love will build them up again and again.

The perfect type of these relations which are the object of all our progress is disclosed to us in the historical life of our Lord. He declares to us the love of God. He shows us what it is to live the life of sonship towards God. He exemplifies the life of a brother among His fellow-men. Lastly, He shows us, through His Kingly leadership, the spectacle of a society knit together in the bonds of a common attachment to their head, and through Him to one another. And all this He has done, not merely in idea, nor in precept, but in actual fact. He has shown us that the thing is possible. "God sending His Son in the likeness of sinful flesh, has condemned sin in the flesh."

Now it might at first seem as if this would lead us simply to go back to the Christ once manifested in history; and, instead of moving hopefully forward, to bend back our energies and cramp our ideas by the circumstances of the life of our Lord. Accordingly, it has been argued that the Incarnation is the very doctrine of immobility, nay, of reaction; that its effect must necessarily be to fill men with a longing for the past, not for the future, to make them timid and sceptical as to all possibility of progress; that the believer in a Christ who has fulfilled all righteousness is a believer in a humanity which has exhausted itself; and that all hopes for the future are thus benumbed beforehand by the belief that they have all been anticipated in the one career of highest excellence, from which all subsequent life must be a decline. We must admit, with sorrow, that Christians have often, by their timid conduct and want of spirit, given too much colour to this supposition. But where they have done so, they have gone in the teeth of the whole teaching of our Lord about the Comforter. Christ's historical life was not meant to be the end. Christ has passed away from the outer

presence that His life may no longer be a law of the
letter to His followers, but that the spirit of His life
may become the spirit of their lives in all their ever-
varying phases.

Christ's life, as disclosed to our hearts by the
Holy Spirit, is a great ideal which is always before
us. We have apprehended it in some sort, but we
are occupied all our life in growing towards it. St.
Paul, while he declared that Christ had become his
righteousness, yet described himself as ever pressing
on towards that righteousness. "That I may be
found in Him," he says, "that I may have the
righteousness which is of God by faith, that I may
know Him and the power of His resurrection. . . .
Forgetting those things which are behind, and reaching forth unto those things which are before, I press
towards the mark."

The life of Christ, again, as brought home to our
souls by the Holy Spirit, is a stimulus to our faculties.
This is the very meaning of the title Comforter—the
supporter and strengthener. "The Lord," says St.
Paul, "is the Spirit." Ὁ Κύριος τὸ πνεῦμά ἐστι. Christ
has, by the gift of the Spirit, become the quickener
of all our independent powers. It is not so much
some new ideal of life which is brought to us from
without ; but rather a gathering up of all that is
good and true in our nature, the constant presenta-
tion of this to the conscience as the object of desire,
and the sustaining of every noble impulse which can
urge us on to attain it. You cannot make use of our

Lord's example or precepts for any other purpose than this. You cannot make Him a mere model or rule to be followed without reference to circumstances and common sense. Those who have tauntingly said that if we believe in Christ we should drive out profane men from our sacred buildings with a scourge, or address our adversaries as serpents and a generation of vipers, have as much travestied the significance of Christ's example as those who choose on Maundy Thursday to wash the feet of a few beggars. And those who see in the words about the tribute money a demand for the separation of men's moral life into two distinct spheres are as mistaken as those who deduce from the Sermon on the Mount the wrongfulness of oaths or of self-defence. It is the spirit, not the letter, of Christ's words and deeds which has to be transferred into our lives.

But when we come seriously to attempt this, who is there that does not feel himself embarked in a course which can only be described as one of constant and illimitable progress? There gleams before us an ideal of personal excellence, the form of a human being who is wholly unselfish, utterly devoted to the truth, to man, to God. What discredit this must throw on our present condition, however good it may have seemed to be; nay, what longing for change, for progress towards better things! We know that we shall be like it one day; but as yet we cannot even conceive that likeness to the full. Yet we know that it is only by contemplating that "idea of the good" that we make any real progress : by this alone we are purified more and more, our spirits are "changed from glory to glory, as by the Lord the Spirit." We trace out an ideal of truth, a state in which we shall gaze on things as they really are, freed from the mists of prejudice. But He that said "I am the truth" has not given us all truth ready-made, but wills that we should follow Him through scenes in which we "see through a glass darkly," and "know nothing yet as we ought to know." We form an ideal of a holy society in which each individual will take his true place; but it is a kingdom which is not of this world, and it must be sought, not *in*, but *across* and *beyond* each stage of human society which inadequately strives to represent it.

The first partakers of the gift of Pentecost saw all the heavens and the earth trembling around them. The whole moral world was in a flux. The solid fabric of Judaism, which had been like the ground beneath men's feet and the firmament above their heads, was giving way on all sides. "I will show wonders in heaven above, and signs in the earth beneath, blood and fire, and vapour of smoke." The first century, much more than the nineteenth, was an era of revolutions. The second outburst of inspired life, in the time of Stephen, went back upon the Old Testament, and saw that also as a scene of constant progress and change. Then came St. Paul, by whose influence the infant community

burst its Jewish swathing bands, and grew into the
Catholic Church. And the Revelation of St. John
and the Epistle to the Hebrews look on to constant
changes, the shaking, not of the earth only, but also
of heaven, that those things alone which cannot be
shaken, the eternal city of God, may remain. The
line of progress which the Apostolic age thus in-
augurated has never been left, though the Church
has often been dragged on rather than advanced,
with its face towards the ever-receding past. It is
the part of true faith to make this progress conscious and resolute : to admit the pain which this
progress necessarily gives, but to cheer us on by
the assurance that it is expedient for us that successive phases, excellent though they may have
seemed, should pass away, and that, if we be but
steadfast and sincere, the true blessedness lies before
us.

Let me apply this to three spheres : 1st, To the
pursuit of truth ; 2ndly, To the constitution of the
Church ; 3rdly, To our personal lives. Progress is
the law in each.

1. It is sometimes doubted whether in theology
proper there is such a thing as progress. On a recent
occasion, of much importance to our branch of the
Church, it was said, with apparent assent on all
sides, that "while science was progressive, and its
interest must go on increasing, theology was of its
very nature stationary, the relations of God with
man standing now in the same position as they did

5,000 years ago."* Is it presumptuous to traverse and
deny that statement, and to believe that new light
must constantly be coming to us so long as God
discloses His purposes by changing circumstances,
and the experience of mankind is constantly growing?
The statement that theology is non-progressive is
only true so far as we wilfully abstract and separate
theology from life, and from other fields of thought;
and I venture to think that the truest progress is
that which is being forced upon us by the constant
demand that we should be real, and that we should
show at every step a connection between the theological conceptions which we propound and the
actual life of men.

A Scotch theologian who spent his short life in
pursuing a higher truth than had been attained by his
countrymen, and died while pursuing it, said that he
thought we might trace in the theology of the last
three centuries a progress corresponding with the
words, "the way," "the truth," and "the life." "The
way," which had been obscured in the middle ages,
was pointed out afresh by the great outburst of light
at the Reformation. Then came the effort to probe
and draw out "the truth," producing detailed and
often conflicting systems; but now we are coming to
view religious truth more simply in its relation to
"life."

* These words were used by Mr. Bruce, now Lord Aberdare, in
the House of Commons, on the occasion of Mr. Miall's motion for
disestablishment.

Is not this the tendency on all hands in the present day? The criticism is often made, and received with much alarm, that there never was an age which more fully believed in the moral side of Christianity, nor one which was less disposed to accept the historical facts or dogmatic statements in which it has been enshrined. I think the criticism is to a large extent true; and it represents, no doubt, a state of some confusion and vacillation. But does it not point us to this—that the first duty of theology in our day is to show its bearing upon life, and that the moral elements are being recognised as the living centre round which all the rest should group themselves? We need not take sides in a supposed conflict between dogmatic theology and the Christian life; but we must imperatively bring them into harmony, and subject all we say about God and Christ to the constant test of a living experience. Let theology begin, not with the creation, but with the life of Jesus of Nazareth; let it lay stress, not primarily on such propositions as these, that God is omniscient, omnipresent, omnipotent, but rather upon these, that God is love, and that Christ is the manifestation of the Divine life of love to men; and then we shall cease to come into collision with the great convictions of mankind; we shall begin at least with having these convictions as our allies. May we not believe that one great work of the Divine Comforter in the present day is to be seen in the inducing of so general a consensus as we witness

P

to the belief that a life of self-renouncing love is the only true life to be lived by man on earth? Hardly a moral writer, of whatever school, nay, hardly a writer of tales of fiction, and hardly a political thinker, but bears witness in some way to this conviction—and this, whether or not they connect this conviction with its true spring in the Cross of Jesus Christ. Why should we not welcome this fact as our chief ally, and, from the circle of light and love which is thus gained to us all in common, endeavour by a united effort to clear up the mysteries which have been expressed by the clashing dogmas of the past?

I am indicating a method, not a system. And, if it be a true one, it implies the most perfect freedom for every form of thought—freedom, I mean, not merely according to laws, but the freedom which comes from mutual trustfulness. We have found a sure and acknowledged standing-ground in the Christian life of self-renouncing love, the reflection of the Cross of Christ. Grounded on this, we need not be so nervously anxious about the rest. Nay, we must expect new light in all departments. And yet, how often do we witness the melancholy fact that one who has some light to give upon some region of truth is met by the question, "Do you, in the ultimate result, hold by this or that received opinion?" and, "if not," it is added, "we will have nothing to say to you." And then the man takes you at your word, and comes to believe that his views inevitably clash with some great received truths, and he is driven into heresy, and you lose the help which you might have gained from him. And, meanwhile, though it is supposed that truth as a system has been the gainer by this barren victory, truthfulness, which is the most marked feature of the Spirit's work, has suffered irretrievably. We want, among educated men such as those whom I now address, more tolerance of opinion, more patience of the bearing of various forms of thought upon the great realities of our existence ; and, at the same time, much more carefulness as to our own sincerity in our dealings and our influence in such matters.

Nay, more. Why should it be the case that the attitude of Christians towards new discoveries should almost always be that of suspicion and timidity ? and that, even when impartial persons are convinced, Christians should often be the last instead of the first to yield to the true conviction ? It indicates, surely, a wrong condition of mind. We smile as we read that Bishop Horne and his friends in the beginning of the last century formed a Society at Oxford for the purpose of resisting on religious grounds the discoveries of Newton. But the aggregate of such attempts should cost us more than a smile. I am ashamed to think that, in reference to the greatest triumphs in political life and in the physical sciences, at almost every stage Christians have been merely driven to acquiesce, and to discover as an afterthought a reconciliation between the new ideas and those which they had advocated. I rejoice in the

P 2

reconciliation, but I am ashamed that there should ever have been the war. The war has arisen from the overvaluing of the outward integuments, the undervaluing of the truth itself. It is time that we should awake, by the constant teachings of experience, from our injurious attitude : that the Church should become, not the check, but the constant and trustful stimulant of the freest thought. Why should we always think that the sphere in which we move is so narrow that we dare not advance lest we should run against the boundaries? May not the boundaries be enlarged? Or rather, are we sure that there are any boundaries at all in the direction in which we are looking? May it not be that what we have taken for the necessary limits of our system is only a certain dimness which will clear away if we go boldly on?

We fear lest some statement which seems to us a pillar of the whole edifice of truth should be overthrown. It is not the statement, but the principle, for which we ought to be jealous. We set out, perhaps, like a distinguished man who has told the history of religious opinions, with insisting that a certain defined body of doctrine or a certain defined order of ministers must somewhere exist, to be the prerequisites of Christian belief and practice ; and when events bring us face to face with the fact that these are the very things which there is grave reason to question, we turn away as from some impious suggestion. Or we are afraid lest to us, as to some especially in Ger-

many, the very centre of all, the life of our Lord on
earth should grow dim, and we shrink back from any
full inquiry into the documents which enshrine it.
And then, at every point, the path of truth is a
rugged one, each step that we make sure leading to a
further step, till we are weary with the pursuit. Can
I not make to myself a resting-place here, or here?
The answer is, that a moral and spiritual, rather than
an intellectual and dogmatic, certitude is that which
God designs for us ; that the form changes and will
change, while the essence of our faith remains the
same ; that, if the path be long and hard, that is but
a trial of our patience and our courage ; aye, that
even if it should be so that the path should lead us
under the shadow of the most terrible doubts, yet the
life of self-sacrificing love, which is the spiritual
centre of the Christian revelation, could never fail us,
and that of this sacrifice the following of truth is the
noblest form ; and yet (for here experience comes to
our aid), that the progress destined for us is one in
which all that is precious to us must be preserved, for
that on which past generations of Christian men have
fed their faith can never be fundamentally false. It
may be that, in that progress, the clear light of the
Saviour's presence may for a time be darkened ; but
a better, a more spiritual, view of Him lies beyond ;
and of these more gloomy parts of our progress, as of
that which the disciples were to make, He would
surely say to us : The change is still expedient ; "ye
now therefore have sorrow ; but I will see you again

and your heart shall rejoice, and your joy no man taketh from you."

2. The same principles must be applied to progress in the Church itself—in the relations of the Christian society towards its own members. Here, too, we are striving to realise an ideal of heavenly love of which the vision is seen for us by St. Paul when he reveals the Church as the Bride of Christ, "not having spot or wrinkle, or any such thing;" and by St. John, in the imagery of the New Jerusalem. It cannot be too emphatically stated that these ideal visions of the Church do not apply to anything now in the world, that each successive phase of Church life is but a faint striving towards them ; and, moreover, that the Christians of each age are left absolutely free to accommodate their institutions from time to time to their special wants, so long as the great ideal is kept practically before their eyes.

Why is it, my brethren, that the Church of Christ, which of all societies in the world contains the most swelling springs of life, should be marked in its history by the constant tendency to lean upon the past—that it has been overlaid by traditional thought and practice, and has had so little of the promised spirit of prophetical prevision ? Why has our progress been marked as much or more than the progress of society in general by convulsive struggles between the parties of order and of movement ? Why, but because we have been unfaithful to the presence of the Spirit amongst us ?

There are some persons, no doubt, whose critical habit is so overweening that hardly any institutions of worship or of government can satisfy them. But ought we on this account to refuse to move forward when the conditions of our life demand change? What is the truth about the various stages through which the Church has to pass? It is this, that each age, for itself, is bound to make a vigorous effort to realise the ideal of the Church, but must still be conscious that all which it can accomplish is but a faint sketch of that ideal, a sketch which it must leave to be filled up or modified by the mature experience of after-times. Not one of the institutions of the past, not even (so far as they may be traced) of the Apostolic age, is binding in its letter upon all after ages. It is, indeed, a noble attempt to which each age is called, to evolve, according to its own wants, and by the light of past experience, such institutions as will best embody the true relations of men to each other, as members of a Christian brotherhood, and their relations to God in worship and in service. And it is necessary to take in the experience and the traditions of the past. But nothing can be more pernicious than the attempt to bind our own ways or those of past ages upon all future generations. The arrangements which we make are, if looked at in view of the whole career of the Church, not like solid houses to remain through centuries, but temporary halting-places. They embody the present convictions of men; but they must needs be altered in a hundred ways, according to the ceaseless changes of the ever-working Spirit which dwells in the Church's heart.

Great respect must be paid, no doubt, to the experience of those who have gone before us, but only so far as their experience really applies to our circumstances. To make quotations from the old Church writers, and apply them immediately to passing events, is for the most part a fallacious process. To quote the decrees of ancient councils on matters as to which the circumstances and the grounds of men's thoughts have changed, is to apply for the most part a misguiding standard. It is the spirit and general attitude of our Christian ancestors, not the letter of their decrees, that will help us in the difficulties of our own time. And when, as often happens, the mere customs of ancient days are brought in to override what is truly expedient now, we are really in danger of forgetting that we live under the dispensation of the Spirit, and that "Where the Spirit of the Lord is, there is liberty."

It can hardly be doubted by those who look soberly into the state of the Church at the present day that great modifications, both of its external and internal relations, are at hand. It is all but impossible that the Church of England should continue long in its present condition. It is a great aristocratic institution, when all other institutions are subject to popular control. It is still governed, in minute points, by the central power, while in all other departments of life discretion is entrusted to local authorities. It is a national institution which, through the helpless perpetuation of an ancient wrong, excludes from its pale nearly one half of the Christian people of this realm, and it is isolated from nine-tenths of Christendom. Whatever form the changes may take which are to remedy these evils, such changes must surely come. But why should we fear to advance boldly and accommodate ourselves to the needs of our generation ? Have not we, as well as former ages, the Spirit of God to lead us ? Is there anything to prevent our using the most entire freedom in adapting ourselves to the altered circumstances of our day ? Are we bound to stigmatise for ever, as schismatics, the members of Christian communities not episcopally governed ? Are we to be debarred from using in the pulpit the services of men not episcopally ordained, because former ages have seldom used them ? Are we to continue to limit our Churches to one particular form of service and of address because it was thought necessary 200 years ago to guard against abuses by laws of uniformity ? Are we to apply in all Church offices a rigid test of adherence to our present system ? Are we to refuse to administer the Holy Communion at the only times when poor people in towns can satisfactorily come, because in past years, under different circumstances, it was thought necessary that it should be received fasting ? Or, again, are we to be hindered by the memory of superstitious abuses from retaining or restoring ancient usages which may be really edifying, from using ancient forms of speech which may best represent the truth, or from seeking union, where there is any practical meaning in it, with the older as well as the newer divisions of the Christian body? It may be that, as some think, we have to pass through a searching ordeal, in which all customs and beliefs will be sifted. Let us enter upon that ordeal in the bold yet reverent spirit of the writer of the Epistle to the Hebrews, who, while he looked forward to the shaking of both earth and heaven, yet knew that this shaking would issue in the greater stability of all that was vital. The ordeal is brought to bear on us, so " That those things which cannot be shaken may remain," for " we receive a Kingdom which cannot be moved."

Are there those here who tremble at the new position made for our universities and colleges by the abolition of religious tests? Let them not look back to the supposed securities which once gone are gone for ever, but hopefully prepare for the time to come. May it not be that greater freedom will throw men more back upon conviction ; that the fact of no formal profession being exacted will bring out more distinctly men's real belief, and that what you lose in seeming you will gain in public sincerity? May it not be that the words of St. Paul, as to the effect of religious differences, may here gain an application, " That they which are approved may be made manifest ;" and that some who have been backward to show their belief, when to do so was to identify themselves with a system of religious ascendancy, may in a more open field take up a positive and assured position ? I cannot but believe that here, too, it will in the end be found that it was expedient that the change should come, and that the abandonment of the old and worn-out system will prove the beginning of a better state.

3. The principle of hopeful and confident progress by the working in us of the Holy Spirit may be applied to our individual lives.

Life is necessarily a progress in the sense that we constantly change. It is a progress necessarily also in the sense that we gain experience as we move on. To make it progress in the true sense, the faith and the hope are needed which come from the consciousness of redemption. Without this, the future is dreary indeed, and no poet of Nature, no Mimnermus or Anacreon, no Byron or Béranger has ever adequately described the real horror of the inevitable passage from youth to age, from vigour of intellect to a second childhood, from the generous hopes of youth to the churlishness of declining life. What is it that can convert the complaints of mankind into a song of triumph ? I know of nothing but the old, old story of the Death and Resurrection and Ascension of our Lord impressed on us by the Holy Spirit ; the assurance that self-sacrificing love, which has sounded the depths of human sin and misery and has not been overcome by them, is supreme in God's universe, and destined to complete dominion. He that has

thus believed has within him a never-failing spring of
hope and joy: and with these comes to us the assurance
that we ourselves shall not be overcome by the cor-
rupting power of selfishness. To conceive this hope
is the truest conversion: to abandon it, the worst
backsliding. To him who holds it fast, life can be
but a progress of many stages towards ever maturer
blessedness.

I engage you, I pledge and bind you over into
this hope, young hearts, whose fresh life is learning to
unfold itself amid the scenes of this University. Hope
is natural to youth. Take heed that your hope is
well grounded ; then it cannot be too fervent or enthusiastic. Look forward with joy, and count each
change that is coming, whatever the momentary pain
which it may bring, to be a passage on to better
things. You have passed through some such stages
already, and you passed into them, perhaps, un-
willingly at the time. But have they not been
fraught with true profit to you ? You passed from
a beloved home, and school seemed strange to you at
first. You wept, perhaps, at the exchange of the
home fireside and the endearments of parents and
sisters for the rougher scenes and companionships of
school. But your school soon became to you, I can
hardly doubt, a place of fresh interest, an arena of
new aspirations. You felt proud of it, and you
regretted it keenly when you came to leave. And
who that has loved his school has not felt his heart
turn back to it with a pang, when as a timid freshman

he has felt his way with doubtful steps among the
large and strange experiences of the University?
But I should think ill of you if I suspected that you
still looked back, and preferred the comparatively
childish ways of the best of schools to the ampler
life, the fuller culture, to which Oxford invites her
sons. He that has entered into one tithe of these
advantages must ever cling with grateful affection to
the place where he first felt the spring of mature
thought and learned with independent resolve to gird
himself for the work of life. Keep your heart fresh,
and your conscience pure, young men. May Oxford
be to you all that it is in the idealising memory of
those who are now growing old.

But will you then, because the present scene is
happy and fruitful, linger here, and shrink from what
is to come? Will you contrast with your studies of
poetry, or history, or philosophy, or with the pleasant
contact of youthful, expansive minds, the crabbedness
of law, the dulness of a curacy, dry business, the
society of common men and women? Will you (I
know that it is the temptation of many) thus discount
the future, thus take the heart out of the coming
time, till evil, selfish forebodings almost create their
own fulfilment? Rather, with Christian hopefulness,
fill the future with the blessed hopes of duty, and the
love of your fellow-men, and the luxury of doing
good. Depend upon it, one half of the dangers of
university life, on which many have to look back
with regret, come from the thoughtless and selfish

spirit which refuses to look forward. They will be conjured away if you make your Oxford career, not a scene of listless satisfaction, but one of serious preparation for the work of your life. The time that lies before you is full of ampler experiences, nobler opportunities; and in the practical life, if our feet are more firmly planted on earth, our minds may yet be nearer heaven. Pass on, young Christian, soberly, but without fear. And if in the larger thoughts which this free republic of the mind has given you the fabric of your ideas has undergone some change, do not think that the future need bring you either an abandonment of aspirations for truth, or a wearing away of faith into negation. Do your duty trustfully, and with prayer; and who is he that will harm you in all the days that are coming?

It is said that men, as they grow older, learn the hollowness of their youth's ideals. I know not why this should be so. That the mere effervescence of the youthful recruit should pass away is natural; but, if the veteran should be more circumspect, he should also be more daring. The first sketch was inadequate; the newer plans should be drawn with a bolder hand. The glorious thoughts that belong to immortality, and the promise of Christ's return, should suggest to us constantly new spheres which the spirit of love may occupy; and, like Ulysses, even in old age we may cry :—

> " Come, my friends,
> Tis not too late to seek a newer world."

Perhaps the greatest hindrance to men in fulfilling the work which they ought to accomplish in life is the want of spiritual enterprise—I had almost said ambition. The man who has had some earnest moments thinks he has saved his soul, and looks back to what he was in the "peaceful hours he once enjoyed," instead of embracing the opportunities of fuller religious life which the coming days are unfolding. The man who has had some success in literature rests on his reputation or works on his old materials, instead of training his genius for higher flights. The man who has been forward in some good cause which has triumphed, looks back to the former scenes of conflict rather than to the wars which have yet to be waged against evil. And those who in youth have been ardent reformers, become upholders of abuses in later life. "Such is the natural course," you say. Natural, no doubt, so far as natural means selfish; but not the Christian course. May the Holy Spirit of God take from us the lethargy and the timidity which so well befit our natural selfishness, and give us the great boldness and freedom which was the heritage of Christ's Apostles. Let us count as among our chief dangers that timorousness which is the parent both of cowardice and of cruelty. Let us advance, expecting, not a renewal of gifts which have passed away, but new gifts suited to our age, fuller light, greater breadth and tolerance as distinctly Christian virtues, more power to adapt social and political circumstances to the work of the Church, fuller sympathy with the needs and aspirations of the masses of our poorer fellow-countrymen, more ability to harmonise the refinements of art, of literature, nay, of humour, with the spiritual and eternal wants of men, and greater simplicity of life, to purify our age from selfish luxury. These, surely, are the gifts for which our generation cries aloud, and these the Comforter is waiting to bestow. Let us ask and we shall receive; and, whether we ourselves succeed or fail, we shall aid the world in its course towards the promised triumph of our Lord.

THE END.

www.ingramcontent.com/pod-product-compliance
Lightning Source LLC
Chambersburg PA
CBHW031424020726
47499CB00005B/1582